W0303788

IP Assets: An Awakening in the Market?

DANIEL MATTES

Copyright © 2019 Daniel Mattes
ISBN: 9781692202231
All rights reserved.

Coverphoto: iStockphoto.com

Images and Graphics:
Daniel Mattes

Author Photo: Private

Graphic Design Supervision and Details:
Atelier Kubinecz, Ilona Braune

Printing and Binding: Print Consult, München
Printed in the EU

Stay informed: https://42.cx
Find us on Facebook and LinkedIn

CONTENT

ACKNOWLEDGMENTS

First, I want to thank my wife, Karolina. Thank you so much, dear.
The world is a better place thanks to people who want to develop and lead others. What makes it even better are people who share the gift of their time to mentor others. Thank you to everyone who strives to grow and help others grow.
To all the individuals I have had the opportunity to lead, be led by, or watch their leadership from afar, I want to say thank you for being the inspiration and foundation for this book.
Without the experiences and support from my team at 42.cx, this book would not exist. A special thank you to our Advisory Board members Jivka, Gabi, Markus and Martin.

SYNOPSIS

The global innovation race is heating up, with advances in artificial intelligence, block chain, biotechnology, data storage and other cutting-edge technologies transforming sectors and global markets. This is also evidenced in the fact that the ratio of tangible to intangible assets of industry leaders around the world has been seeing a drastic change over the past four decades. The market capitalization of the S&P 500 is currently made up of 84% intangible assets, up from 20% in 1975 (according to MSCI). In this book, we demonstrate that analysing intangible assets of a company in great detail allows building models to accurately forecast a company's ability to convert its intellectual property into stock value in the following quarters. We also demonstrate that a company's AI-IP impact correlates significantly with its future stock returns.

Our book offers a new innovation-related measure, IPI, which is contemporaneously associated with market valuation and predicts future operating performance and stock returns. Existing studies relating to innovation and market performance focus on the effects of either the input (R&D) or the output (patents) of innovation separately. Our study differs in focusing on Artificial Intelligence based innovative efficiency as a ratio of innovative output to input, based on the idea that efficiency should be highly value relevant. We find that the predictive power of AI innovation is incremental to that of other innovation related variables such as R&D intensity, significant R&D growth, patent counts and citations.

We demonstrate that portfolio analysis confirms our hypothesis and show that a portfolio of top companies generated a return of 237% (+159% to baseline), which is significantly higher than the market (+78%).

1. INTRODUCTION

The global innovation race is heating up, with advances in artificial intelligence, block chain, biotechnology, data storage and other cutting-edge technologies transforming sectors and global markets. To compete, companies can innovate in-house, or they can acquire others' innovations. This is also evidenced in the fact that the ratio of tangible to intangible assets of industry leaders around the world has been seeing a drastic change over the past four decades. As these technological advances began driving innovation, the size and diversity within company asset portfolios began increasing consistently. This dramatic shift is evident in the market capitalization of S&P 500 in 2015, which was made up of 84% intangible assets, as noted by MSCI. In 1975, intangible assets only made up less than 20% of the total asset value.

Figure 1:

S&P 500 MARKET VALUE

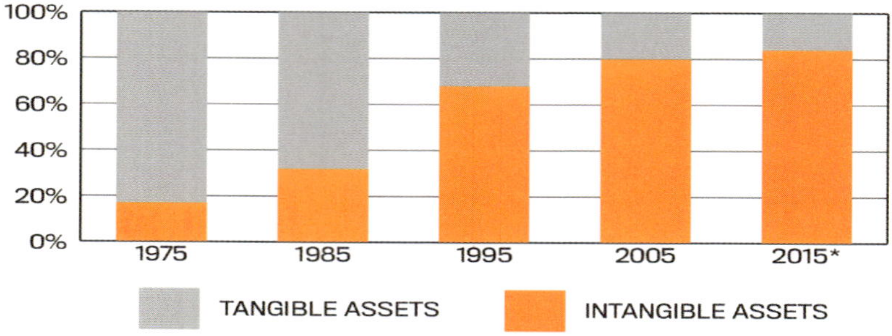

Source: Ocean TOMO, LLC
*January 1, 2015

However, investors devote considerable attention to analyst reports, fundamental data, earning calls or news articles, while intangible assets receive less attention. Evidence exists that individuals pay less attention to, and place less weight upon, information that is harder to process. Information about intangible assets and innovation is hard to process, because it requires developing and applying a theory of how the economic fundamentals of a firm or its industry are changing. It also requires an analysis of the quality and path from intellectual property & inventions to final products on the market, the profit of which can be highly uncertain and long deferred.

In such a situation, where a majority of the S&P 500 is in intangible assets, it is only prudent to be employing the best in class techniques for research and benchmarking, to ensure that decisions are based on data of the highest quality.

In such a situation, where a majority of the S&P 500 is in intangible assets, it is only prudent to be employing the best in class techniques for research and benchmarking, to ensure that decisions are based on data of the highest quality.

Lauren Cohen et. al have demonstrated in a Harvard research book that the stock market is unable to distinguish between "good" and "bad" R&D investment, despite the fact that successful innovation is in fact predictable. They found that the market consistently misvalues information in an ex-ante, predictable way. Specifically, the market does not take into account the information in firms' past R&D abilities. Firms that have been successful in the past and that invest heavily in R&D as percentage of sales earn substantially higher future stock returns than firms that invest identical amounts in R&D, but have poor past track records.

Over the last decades, the analysis of company patent portfolios has become an increasingly important part of competitive intelligence activities, as well as a key tool in analysing national, regional, and company technology strengths. Implicit in these analyses is the idea that identifying a company's intellectual assets, specifically those intangible assets that patents protect, is tantamount to identifying areas of strength within a company. Given the rise and exponential growth of Artificial Intelligence technology, the focus on Artificial Intelligence related intellectual property is key to a company's future growth and success. Companies with focus on Artificial Intelligence are two times more likely to grow exponentially than companies without.

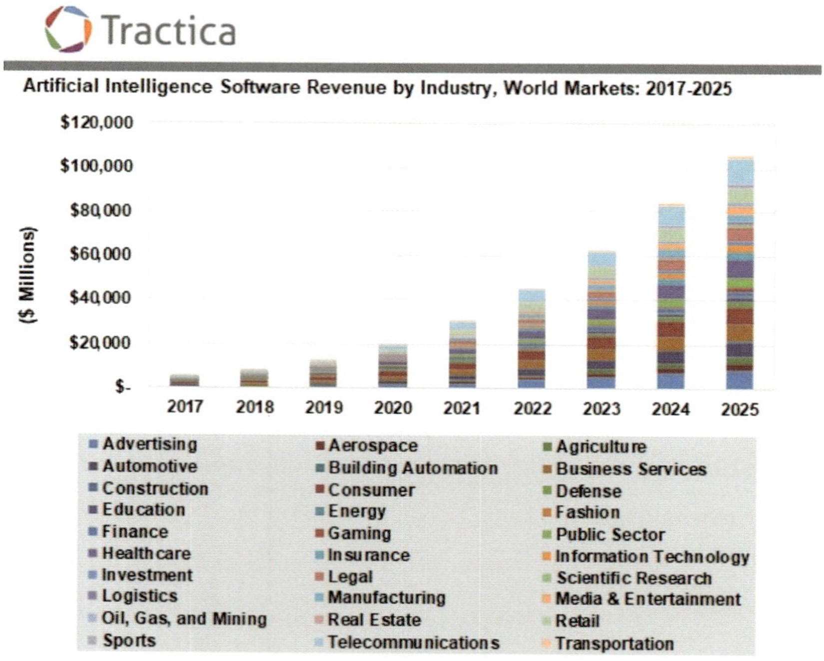

Source: Tractica

In addition, the environment for innovation and technology has become more and more complex and difficult to analyse, especially with technologies emerging in the field of Artificial Intelligence. According to the market research firm Tractica, the global artificial intelligence software market is expected to experience massive growth in the coming years, with revenues increasing from around 9.5 billion U.S. dollars in 2018 to an expected 118.6 billion by 2025. The overall AI market includes a wide array of applications such as natural language processing, robotic process automation, and machine learning.

We can also assert that the rise of Artificial Intelligence is a global phenomenon. 83 percent of 2017 AI books on Scopus originate outside the U.S.. 28 percent of these books originate in Europe — the largest percentage of any region. University course enrolment in artificial intelligence (AI) and machine learning (ML) is increasing all over the world, most notably at Tsinghua in China, whose combined AI + ML 2017 course enrolment was 16x that of 2010. And there is progress beyond just the United States, China, and Europe. South Korea and Japan were the 2nd and 3rd largest producers of AI patents in 2014, after the U.S. Additionally, South Africa hosted the second Deep Learning Indaba conference, one of the world's largest ML teaching events, which drew over 500 participants from 20+ African countries.

There is a growing awareness that the Artificial Intelligence intellectual property owned by companies can be an important factor in their commercial success. Intellectual property, particularly in the form of patents, provides the technological foundation upon which new products and services are built. Background research provides a strong rationale for the expectation that companies with strong IP portfolios, especially with intellectual in the Artificial Intelligence segment, will perform better in the stock market. A method devised to accurately measure the quality of company technology and innovation should therefore have a significant predictive effect on company stock performance.

Furthermore, information of this type should be particularly valuable because it is not currently available to market analysts, leading to the strong assumption that the quality of company technology might not be properly valued in the market. Deng et al. showed that companies with high-quality patent portfolios had market-to-book valuations that were 25 percent higher than other companies in the same industries with lesser-quality portfolios, both contemporaneously and for a number of years in the future.

The activity at the heart of our investigation is investment in research and development (R&D) combined with the strength and impact of its intellectual property, especially its Artificial Intelligence intellectual property (AI-IP). Given that R&D stimulates innovation and technology change, which can in turn lead to improvements in productivity, living standards and economic output, the quality of R&D investment and the ability to turn AI-IP into revenues and profitability is a critical task of the market.

In this book, we demonstrate that analysing intangible assets of a company in great detail allows building a model to accurately forecast a company's ability to convert its intellectual property into stock value in the following quarter. We also demonstrate that a company's AI-IP impact correlates significantly with its future stock returns.

Our findings add to a growing amount of literature highlighting the market's inability to properly value investments in R&D. An alternative argument for why innovative efficiency would predict higher future returns derives from the q-theory (Cochrane, 1991, 1996; Liu Whited and Zhang, 2009). Firms with higher innovative efficiency tend to be more profitable and have higher returns on assets.

All else equal, the q-theory implies that higher profitability predicts higher returns because a high return on assets indicates that these assets were purchased by the firm at a discount (i.e. that they carry a high-risk premium). Specifically, suppose that the market for capital being purchased by a firm is competitive and efficient. When a firm makes an R&D expenditure to purchase innovative capital, the price it pays is appropriately discounted for risk. For concreteness, we can think, for example, of a firm that acquires a high-tech target at a competitive market price. In this scenario, a firm on average achieves higher return (large number of patents, resulting in high cash flows) on its innovative expenditures as fair compensation if its purchased innovative capital is highly risky, and it receives low return if capital is relatively low-risk. Past innovation efficiency is, therefore, a proxy for risk, so firms that have high past innovative efficiency should subsequently be productive in patenting (Dierickx and Cool, 1989) and earn higher profits and stock returns. In other words, q-theory also predicts a positive innovative efficiency return relation.

2. SCIENTIFIC BACKGROUND

Bronwyn H. Hall from the National Bureau of Economic Research (NBER) is one of the pioneers in researching correlations between intangible assets, patents and market value. In their NBER working paper "Market Value and Patent Citations: A First Look" they explore the contributions of R&D spending, patents, and citation-weighted patents to measures of Tobin's Q for the firms. They used a new and comprehensive dataset containing over 4800 U. S. Manufacturing firms and their patenting activity for the past 30 years and find that citation-weighted patent stocks are more highly correlated with market value than patent stocks themselves and that this fact is due mainly to the high valuation placed on firms that hold very highly cited patents.

They found that forward patent citations are in important proxy to measure the importance and impact of a patent:

- **More valuable patents are cited more often;**
- **One quarter of patents receive no citations;**
- **0.01% receive more than one hundred citations;**
- **Lag distribution is skew to the left with a mode at about 3.5 years. (Most cites happen by 10 years, but there can be long lags up to 30 years); and**
- **Number per patent has increased recently with the advent of computerized search.**

Hall and her team performed a large firm level study, which relates market-book value ratio to stock of R&D spending, average patent yield per R&D and average cite yield per patent. They found that cites per patent are more important than the number of patents itself: an increase of one forward cite per patent led to an increase of 3% in market value, a remarkable result. They also identified two major problems for research: Inconsistent assignee names and no common register of assignees (even within the patent offices) are making it difficult to cluster and match patent data to companies. With huge human effort, they matched 3 million U.S. patents granted between 1963 and 2002 to a Compustat database of all firms traded in the U.S. stock market and also collected over 16 million citations made to these patents between 1975 and 2002.

New machine learning technologies, specifically Natural Language Processing (NLP) could mostly automate these tasks today and become a valuable source of information.

2.1 OECD INDICATORS

In an effort to standardize the measurement of patent quality, the OECD issued its paper "Measuring Patent Quality: Indicators of Technological and Economic Value". It proposes a wide array of indicators capturing the technological and economic value of patented inventions, and the possible impact that these might have on subsequent technological developments. The measures proposed build extensively upon recent literature, rely on information contained in the patent documents, and are calculated on patent cohorts defined by the combination of the technology field and the year of filing of patents. This is done to account for possible time- and technology-related shocks.

The proposed patent quality measures aim to facilitate analysis both at the level of the individual patent and at the aggregate patent portfolio level. They are intended to help addressing a number of policy-relevant questions, for example, related to: firms innovation strategies and performance; enterprise dynamics, including the drivers of enterprise creation and of mergers and acquisitions; the determinants of productivity; the financing of innovative enterprises; the output of R&D activities and the returns to R&D investments; the depreciation of R&D; the output of universities and of public research organisations.

- **Patent scope index**

The scope of patents is often associated with the technological and economic value of patents. Lerner (1994) observes that the technological breadth of patents in a firm's portfolio significantly affects the valuation of the firm, and that broad patents are more valuable when many possible substitutes in the same product class are available. Matutes, Régibeau and Rockett (1996) also look at patent protection regimes, and in particular at the length and scope4 of patent protection, and suggest that the scope of a patent should be used to foster the early disclosure of fundamental innovations.

The index proposed in the paper follows Lerner (1994) and defines the scope of a patent in terms of the number of distinct 4-digit subclasses of the International Patent Classification5 the invention is allocated to.

- **Patent family size index**

Owing to the Paris Convention (1883), applicants have up to 12 months from the first filing of a patent application (typically in the country of origin) to file applications in other jurisdictions regarding the same invention and claim the priority date of the first application. The set of patents filed in several countries which are related to each other by one or several common priority filings is generally known as patent family. The value of patents is held to be associated with the geographical scope of patent protection, that is, with the number of jurisdictions in which patent protection has been sought (Lanjouw et al., 1998) and large international patent families have been found to be particularly valuable (Harhoff et al., 2003). Applicants might be willing to accept additional costs and delays of extending protection to other countries only if they deem it worthwhile.

The size of patent families is proxied in the paper by the number of patent offices at which a given invention has been protected. Because of differences in the legal procedures of offices worldwide, and of the delays that these might determine, patent family related indicators may suffer from timeliness. The family size index presented here has been normalised with respect to the maximum value exhibited by other patents in the same cohort, with cohorts that are determined by the pair technology–year.

- **Grant lag index**

Recent evidence (Harhoff and Wagner, 2009; Régibeau and Rockett, 2010) suggests the existence of an inverse relationship between the value of a patent and the length of the grant lag period - defined as the time elapsed between the filing date of the application and the date of the grant. This literature puts forward a revealed preference argument whereby applicants try to accelerate the grant procedure for their most valuable patents, e.g. by means of well documenting their applications and following closely the work of the patent office. Harhoff and Wagner (2009) find that more controversial claims lead to slower grants and that well-documented applications are approved faster. In addition Régibeau and Rockett (2010) suggest that the time required to reach a granting decision depends on the effort made by the filing party, and remark the importance of accounting for the position of patents in the technology cycle. They conclude that important patents are approved more quickly, and the granting delay decreases as industries move from the early stage of their innovation cycle to later stages. Anecdotal evidence gathered from patent examiners tends to support such empirical findings. The grant lag index they propose builds on these recent insights. It relies on patents that are stratified by year and technology field.

- **Backward citations index**

In order to evaluate the novelty of the innovation seeking patent protection, patent applicants are asked to disclose the prior knowledge on which they have relied. This entails listing the possible patents, scientific work and other sources of knowledge at the basis of the invention. Such references, also called backward citations, are then checked by the patent examiner during the technical examination. They can be integrated by means of citing additional relevant prior art, or otherwise removed, if deemed unrelated to the invention under exam (see Alcacer and Gittelman, 2006, in this respect).

Backward citations are used to assess an invention's patentability and define the legitimacy of the claims stated in the patent application (OECD, 2009). At the EPO, backward citations are classified according to their relevance for the patent under exam. Of particular importance are “X” and “Y” citations, as they may question the inventive step of the filed patent (X references if taken alone; Y references if combined with others).

Indicators based on the number of citations made in a patent can help assess the degree of novelty of an invention and investigate knowledge transfers in terms of citations networks (see e.g. Criscuolo and Verspagen, 2008). In addition, aggregating citation data at the country, technology or firm level may be informative of the dynamics of the inventive process. Controlling for self-citations - i.e. citations made to inventions belonging to the same agent – further allows assessing the technological cumulativeness of a firm, i.e. the extent to which new inventions rely on the company’s prior innovative activities. Backward citations either to the patent or to non-patent literature (e.g. scientific papers) have been found to be positively related to the value of a patent (Harhoff et al., 2003). However, large numbers of backward citations may signal the innovation to be more incremental in nature (Lanjouw and Schankerman, 2001)6. Finally, it is worth remarking that, as citation practices and disclosure rules may differ across patent offices, indicators compiled from alternative data sources are generally not comparable.

The number of backward citations per patent is normalised according to the maximum value received by patents in the same year-and-technology cohort. References to non-patent literature have been excluded from the count, whereas self-citations have not.

- **Citations to non-patent literature (NPL) index**

Most patent applications include a list of references – citations – to earlier patents and to non-patent literature (NPL), e.g. scientific papers that set the boundaries of patents' claims for novelty, inventive activity and industrial applicability. Non-patent literature consists of peer-reviewed scientific papers, conference proceedings, databases (e.g. DNA structures, gene sequences, chemical compounds, etc.) and other relevant literature. References are added to reflect the prior art that inventions have built upon. Backward citations to NPL can be considered as indicators of the contribution of public science to industrial technology (Narin et al., 1997).

They may reflect how close a patented invention is to scientific knowledge and help depict the proximity of technological and scientific developments (Callaert et al., 2006). Cassiman et al. (2008) suggest that patents that cite science (i.e. NPL) may contain more complex and fundamental knowledge, and this in turn may influence the generality of patents. Branstetter (2005) further finds that patents citing NPL are of significantly higher quality than patents that do not cite scientific literature.

- **Claims index**

Claims determine the boundaries of the exclusive rights of a patent owner, given that only the technology or aspects covered in the claims can be legally protected and enforced. The number and content of the claims thus determine the breadth of the rights conferred by a patent (OECD, 2009). Moreover, as the structure of the patent fee is generally based on the number of claims contained in the document, a large number of claims might also imply higher fees. Hence, the number of claims in a patent document may not only reflect the technological breadth of a patent, but also its expected market value: the higher the number of claims, the higher the expected value of the patent (Tong and Davidson, 1994; Lanjouw and Schankerman, 2001,7 2004).

They propose a claim-based indicator that relies on EPO patent data stratified by year of filing and technology field. They further construct an indicator of the number of claims over backward citations. They do so following Lanjouw and Schankerman (2001b), who suggest that backward citations are a sign that a patent belongs to a relatively well-developed technology area, and that property rights are less uncertain. For brevity, they call this latter index the "adjusted" index.

- **Forward citations index**

The number of citations a given patent receives (forward citations) mirrors the technological importance of the patent for the development of subsequent technologies, and also reflects, to a certain extent, the economic value of inventions (see Trajtenberg, 1990; Hall, et al., 2005; Harhoff et al., 2003). The guidelines for examination in the European Patent Office require that the references to prior art are classified according to their relevance for the patent application in question. While prior art can be cited as documents defining the non-infringing state of the art in a technology field, there also exist three types of citations that restrict the patentability of a patent application. These are:

- **X citations: documents that are particularly important when taken alone, to the point that a claimed invention cannot be considered novel;**

- **I citations: documents that are particularly important when taken alone, to the point that a claimed invention cannot be considered to involve an inventive step;**

- **Y citations: documents that are particularly relevant if combined with one or more documents of the same category, as such a combination would be obvious to a person skilled in the art.**

Forward citation counts presented here are based on EPO patents citations and take into account patent equivalents – that is, patent documents protecting the same invention at several patent offices (see Webb et al., 2005).

- **Breakthrough inventions index**

Breakthrough inventions are high-impact innovations, which serve as a basis for future technological developments, new products or services. Breakthrough inventions have been found to be strongly associated with entrepreneurial strategies and with further technological development, and are at the centre of many recent studies.

Ahuja and Lampert (2001) explore the relationship between the organisation of established firms and the creation of breakthrough inventions. To this end, they define breakthrough inventions as the top 1% of cited patents (i.e. the most highly cited patents) and find that three organisation-related "traps" generally hinder breakthrough inventions: the familiarity, the maturity and the propinquity traps. Srivastava and Gnyawali (2011) investigate the tension between value creation and value protection, and find that the quality and diversity of the technological resources of a firm are positively correlated with breakthrough innovations. Kerr (2010) relies on Ahuja and Lampert's definition of breakthrough invention in order to investigate the speed at which clusters of technology-related inventions migrate spatially in the aftermath of breakthrough inventions. He finds evidence in support of significantly higher patenting growth in cities and technologies where breakthrough inventions have occurred. Finally, Popp at al. (2012) analyse the return to R&D in some energy technology sectors and find, among other results, that high quality (i.e. breakthrough) patents may induce subsequent innovations in those sectors.

They follow here the definition of breakthrough invention à la Ahuja and Lampert, i.e. as the top 1% cited patents. Similarly to the way in which the different forward citation indicators have been constructed, breakthrough inventions may also be identified by means of restricting the type of citations considered to those coded as X, I and Y.

- **Generality index**

Forward patent citations can be used to assess the range of later generations of inventions that have benefitted from a patent, by means of measuring the range of technology fields – and consequently industries - that cite the patent (Bresnahan and Trajtenberg, 1995). The patent generality index à la Trajtenberg et al. (1997) has been used in a variety of studies aimed to e.g. identify general purpose technologies (Hall and Trajtenberg, 2004); investigate the role of universities as sources of commercial technologies (Henderson et al., 1998); study participation and rent sharing in patent pools (Layne-Farrar and Lerner, 2011); and understand the functioning of the market for innovation and the way patent rights are enforced (Galasso et al, 2011).

The patent generality index proposed in the paper is based on a modification of the Hirschman-Herfindahl Index (HHI) and relies on information concerning the number and distribution of citations received (forward citations) and the technology classes (IPC) of the patents these citations come from. Differently from the way in which generality has been calculated in previous studies (e.g. Hall et al, 2001b) they consider all IPC classes contained in the citing patent documents and account for the number and distribution of both 4-digit and n-digit IPC technology classes contained in citing patents, where n refers to the highest level of disaggregation possible (e.g. A61K 31/5575). Citation measures are built on EPO patents and patent equivalents have been consolidated with. Forward citations cover all categories of citations, and are restricted to a 5-year citation window.

- **Originality index**

Patent originality refers to the breadth of the technology fields on which a patent relies. The patent originality measure, first proposed by Trajtenberg et al. (1997), operationalises this concept of knowledge diversification and its importance for innovation: inventions relying on a large number of diverse knowledge sources are supposed to lead to original results (i.e. on patents belonging to a wide array of technology fields). Patent originality has been used in a wide range of studies, e.g. on the creation of venture-backed start-ups (Gompers et al., 2005); the duration and outcome of the patent examination procedure at the European Patent Office (Harhoff and Wagner, 2009); and the value of post-merger patents vis-à-vis pre-merger ones (Stahl, 2010).

The construction of the patent originality indicator follows a logic that is very similar to the one used to construct the generality index, the main difference being that generality measures rely on forward citations, whereas originality relies on backward cites. The specification proposed in the paper further differentiates the generality and the originality indicators, as the former accounts for the distribution of 7- digit subclasses within the 4 digit classes they belong to, as well as for the distribution of the 4-digit classes contained in citing documents; whereas the latter only accounts for the distribution of citations made at the 4-digit (or 7-digit, in the alternative specification proposed) level.

- **Radicalness index**

Although the concept of radicalness may appear intuitive and easy to grasp, as it evokes something completely different from what exists, defining and measuring the technological radicalness of inventions remains challenging. An index of patent radicalness has been proposed by Shane (2001), where the radicalness of a patent is measured as a time invariant count of the number of IPC technology classes in which the patents cited by the given patent are, but in which the patent itself is not classified. He argues that the more a patent cites previous patents in classes other than the ones it is in, the more the invention should be considered radical, as it builds upon paradigms that differ from the one to which it is applied.

This definition has been adapted in their paper to account for the relative weight of each 4-digit technology class contained in the cited patents. The indicator has further been normalised with respect to the total number of IPC classes listed in the backward citations, so that its value ranges from zero to one. This entails that the overall number of citations, i.e. the denominator of the index, corresponds to the count of citations at the most disaggregated level available, e.g. H05B 41/231. The numerator instead reflects the number of the IPC 4-digit classes contained in the cited documents, weighted by the times these classes appear at the more disaggregated level.

- **Patent renewal index**

The renewal of a patent signals that the invention described in the patent document is still useful, i.e. that it has some value, as no rational agent would be willing to pay money for a right that is worthless.

Information about the renewal of patents has been used in a wide array of studies, which generally suggest that more valuable patents are renewed for longer periods (e.g. Pakes, 1986). Following the pioneering work of Pakes and Schankerman (1984), patent renewal data have been used to estimate the private value of patent protection. These models rely on the assumption that patent owners make profit- maximising renewal decisions, and that patent renewals' rates can be used to estimate the private value of patent protection. Patent renewals' data have also been used to weight patent counts, and to obtain more precise measures of innovative output.

This is the path followed by e.g. Lanjouw, Pakes and Putnam (1998), who hold that more valuable inventions generate larger and/or longer lived patent families. More recently, Svensson (2012) investigates the relationship that exists between the commercialisation and the renewal of patents, and finds a positive correlation between commercialisation and the use of patents for defensive purposes on the one hand and patent renewal on the other hand. He further finds that the quality of patents influences both commercialisation and renewal decisions.

The OECD patent renewal indicator corresponds to the simple count of years during which a granted patent has been kept alive, i.e. the latest year in which it has been renewed or until it has lapsed or has been withdrawn. Years are counted starting from the year in which a patent has been applied.

- **Patent quality: composite index**

Patent quality indicators try to capture both the technological and the economic value of innovations, and are typically based on patent citations, claims, patent renewals and patent family size. They are considered meaningful measures of research productivity and are found to be correlated with the social and private value of the patented inventions. The difference in average patent quality across firms is generally associated with the market evaluation of firms.

The patent quality indicator presented in their paper is an experimental one and may be subject to further refinement. The patent quality index is a composite indicator based on four to six dimensions of patents' underlying quality: forward citations; patent family size; number of claims; generality index; plus backward citations and grant lag. It builds on Lanjouw and Shankerman (2004) and incorporates the generality measure, and a measure accounting for the length of the examination process (i.e. the grant lag index). All components are normalised according to patent cohorts stratified by year and technological field and are given equal importance (no weights).

Three alternative definitions of the experimental patent quality indicator are proposed, in order to better see the impact of the grant lag index and the backward citations index on the indicator:

i. Patent quality index 4 – 4 components: number of forward citations (up to 5 years after publication); patent family size; number of claims; and the patent generality index. Only granted patents are covered by the index.

ii. Patent quality index 4b – 4 components, bis: number of forward citations (up to 5 years after publication); patent family size; corrected claims; and the patent generality index. Only granted patents are covered by the index.

iii. Patent quality index 6 – 6 components: covers the same components as above, plus the number of backward citations and the grant lag index.

2.2 HARVARD'S GOOD & BAD R&D

Lauren Cohen from Harvard Business School and NBER, Karl Diether from the Tuck School of Business at Dartmouth College and Christopher Malloy from Harvard Business School and NBER tested the correlation between research and development (R&D) expenses to sales revenues of a firm. In their paper "Misvaluing Innovation", they demonstrate that a firm's ability to innovate is predictable, persistent, and relatively simple to compute, and yet the stock market ignores the implications of past successes when valuing future innovation. They show that two firms that invest the exact same in research and development (R&D) can have quite divergent, but predictably divergent, future paths.

Their approach is based on the simple premise that while future outcomes associated with R&D investment are uncertain, the past track records of firms may give insight into their potential for future success. They show that a long-short portfolio strategy that takes advantage of the information in past track records earns abnormal returns of roughly 11 percent per year. Importantly, these past track records also predict divergent future real outcomes in patents, patent citations, and new product innovations.

The activity at the heart of their investigation is investment in research and development (R&D). Given that R&D stimulates innovation and technological change, which can in turn lead to improvements in productivity, living standards, and economic output, the proper allocation of R&D investment in the economy is a critical task of the market. And yet, this task is made difficult by the fact that R&D investment is such a highly uncertain activity. Perhaps as a result of this uncertainty, R&D investment has increasingly become a market-driven activity. Although the share of R&D as a percentage of GDP has remained roughly constant (between 2-3%) since the 1960s, the composition of R&D investment in the economy has shifted dramatically, away from federal spending and toward private sector spending. Since the late 1980s, for example, virtually all of the increases in total R&D spending have come from the private sector. The market's role in allocating R&D investment has become more important than ever.

Their empirical strategy proceeds from the notion that past track records represent one simple way to gauge the future prospects of firms. Some firms are skilled at certain activities, and some are not, and this skill may be persistent over time. Using this idea as the starting point for their analysis, they examine the predictability of firm-level R&D investment track records for future returns and future real outcomes. They find that although R&D success is predictable, persistent, and relatively simple to compute, the market largely ignores the information embedded in past track records.

Their identification of past R&D success is based on a simple framework of using a firm's past ability in translating R&D into something the firm values. They then take this "ability" of a firm at R&D and interact it with the amount of research the firm is actually undertaking. For instance, they examine the outcomes of those firms that have been quite good at R&D and are investing heavily in R&D with firms investing identical amounts in R&D, but that have poor past track records. If the market correctly takes into account the prior track records' implications for future success, then whether firms are optimally choosing levels of R&D or not, the market should impound relevant information regarding innovation into prices.

In fact, the market could even be completely incorrect in impounding the impact of every firm's R&D expenditures (as they do have uncertain effects on future firm value), but this would still have no implication for predictability based on past information, as the market will sometimes overvalue and sometimes undervalue this innovation.

They find that the market consistently misvalues innovation in an ex-ante, predictable way. Specifically, the market does not take into account the information in firms' past R&D abilities. Firms that have been successful in the past and that invest heavily in R&D as a percentage of sales ("GoodR&D" firms) earn substantially higher future stock returns than firms that invest identical amounts in R&D, but that have poor past track records ("BadR&D" firms). A portfolio of GoodR&D firms earns equal- and value-weighted excess returns of 135 basis points per month (t=2.76) and 122 basis points per month (t=2.61), and 4-factor alphas of 90 basis points per month (t=3.11) and 78 basis points per month (t=2.27), respectively. In contrast, the portfolio of firms with poor past track records but that invests the same amount of R&D (BadR&D) earns -15 basis points per month in 4-factor value-weighted alpha (t=0.56). The spread portfolio that takes identical high R&D-level portfolios, but exploits differences in past track records, has a 4-factor alpha of 93 basis points per month (t=2.30) or over 11% per year. Returns to the "GoodR&D" (and spread) portfolios are large and significant in the first year, and then returns remain slightly positive but basically plateau in the second and third years, with no reversal. This suggests that we are not capturing a form of overreaction, but instead that the embedded information regarding innovation that the market is misvaluing is important for fundamental firm value.

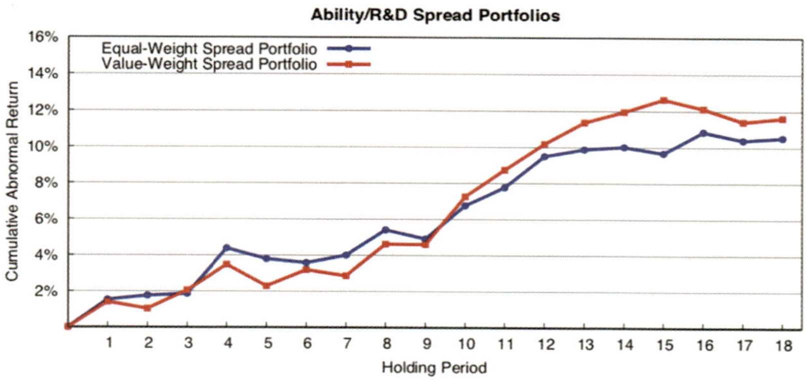

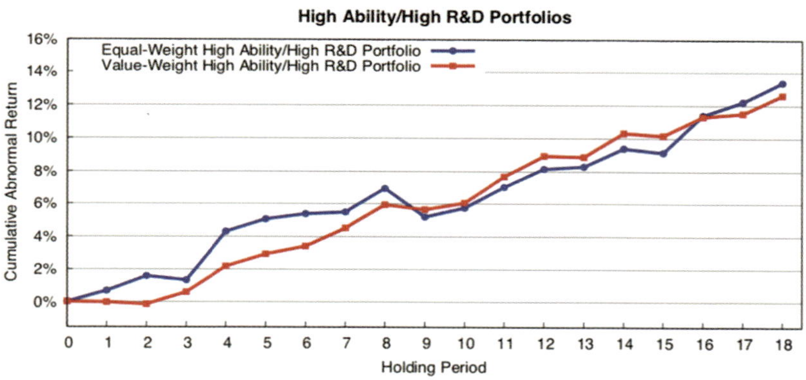

This figure shows the size-B/M-mom adjusted cumulative abnormal returns to portfolios that follow high Ability/high R&D and low Ability/high R&D firms in the 18 months following formation. Each month stocks with positive lagged R&D and non-missing lagged Ability are double sorted into portfolios using quintiles for Ability and 30%/40%/30% breakpoints for R&D. The R&D (Ability estimate) used to form the portfolios is the R&D (Ability estimate) from the fiscal year ending in calendar year t-1 from July to December and calendar year t-2 from January to June (as in Fama and French (1993)). R&D is scaled by sales. Ability is computed as described in Table II. The high Ability/high R&D (low Ability/high R%D) portfolio is formed from the intersection of the top 20% (bottom 20%) of ability and top 30% of R&D. The top graph shows the abnormal return spread between high Ability/high R&D and low Ability/high R&D portfolios. The bottom graph shows the abnormal return on the high Ability/high R&D portfolio. abnormal returns are computed by adjusting returns using 125 size/book-to-market/momentum portfolios (formed as in DGTW (1997)). The sample period is July 1980 to December 2009.

Their findings add to a growing literature highlighting the market's inability to properly value investments in R&D. On one hand, some researchers argue that investors may overestimate the benefits from R&D or simply ignore the fact that many R&D investments are not profitable (Jensen (1993)), leading to the overpricing of R&D- intensive firms. For example, Lakonishok, Shleifer, and Vishny (1994) find that growth stocks earn low future returns, while Daniel and Titman (2006) show that this growth stock underperformance is concentrated in stocks with significant "intangible" information, consistent with market overreaction to intangible information that is difficult to interpret. However, the recent evidence on firm-level R&D activity suggests that, if anything, the market appears to underreact to the information contained in R&D investments.

For example, Chan, Lakonishok, and Sougiannis (2001) and Lev and Sougiannis (1996) demonstrate that firms with high ratios of R&D relative to market equity earn high subsequent returns; Eberhart et al. (2004) find that large increases in R&D expenditures predict positive future abnormal returns; and Hirshleifer et al. (2010) show that firm-level innovative "efficiency" (measured as patents scaled by R&D) forecasts future returns. They show that their results are unaffected by the inclusion of these measures in their tests, and are roughly 3 times larger in magnitude than the findings in, for example, Eberhart et al. (2004) and Hirshleifer et al. (2010), suggesting that their approach is picking up a new and previously undetected pattern in the cross-section of stock returns associated with the market's misvaluation of high R&D ability firms.

Lastly, they run a series of tests designed to pinpoint the mechanism behind their results. First, they explore real outcomes associated with their high R&D ability firms. Specifically, they show that the firms that they classify as high ability firms and that invest heavily in R&D also produce tangible results with their research and development efforts. They generate significantly more patents, achieve significantly more patent-citations, and develop significantly more new products than firms that invest the same levels of R&D, but have poor track records. In addition, they demonstrate that high ability firms exhibit significant persistence in R&D skill, that this skill may be positively related to the presence of a founder, and that the market's failure to understand the implications of R&D track records is related to heterogeneity in information provision by firms.

For example, they show that the predictability in future returns is significantly lower for high ability firms who provide more earnings guidance; under the assumption that firms that provide more earnings guidance are also likely to provide more information to investors more generally (as in Jones (2007)), these findings suggest that cross-sectional variation in information opacity may help explain why the market fails to properly understand the information embedded in firms' past track records.

2.3 INNOVATIVE EFFICIENCY

Similar to Harvard's approach discussed above, David Hirshleifer from the University of California, Po-Hsuan Hsu from the University of Hong Konk and Dongmei Li from the University of California, investigated the correlation between R&D (input) and patents (output). In their paper "Innovative efficiency and stock returns" they find that innovative efficiency (IE), patents or citations scaled by research and development expenditures, is a strong positive predictor of future returns after controlling for firm characteristics and risk. The IE-return relation is associated with the loading on a mispricing factor, and the high Sharpe ratio of the Efficient Minus Inefficient (EMI) portfolio suggests that mispricing plays an important role. Further tests based upon attention and uncertainty proxies suggest that limited attention contributes to the effect. The high weight of the EMI portfolio return in the tangency portfolio suggests that IE captures incremental pricing effects relative to well-known factors.

In this study, they examine the relation between innovative efficiency and subsequent operating performance as well as stock returns. By innovative efficiency, they mean a firm's ability to generate patents and patent citations per dollar of research and development (R&D) investment. The denominator, R&D, measures resource input to innovation. Patents and citations are measures of innovative output, because innovations are usually officially introduced to the public in the form of approved patents. US firms have increasingly recognized the necessity to patent their innovations and, hence, have been especially active in patenting activities since the early 1980s (Hall and Ziedonis, 2001; Hall, 2005) owing to the creation of the Court of Appeals for the Federal Circuit in 1982 and several well-documented patent lawsuits (e.g., the Kodak-Polaroid case). Patents are thus the most important measure of contemporary firms' innovative output (Griliches, 1990), and they are actively traded in intellectual property markets (Lev, 2001).

A firm's past innovative efficiency can be less salient to investors than explicitly forward-looking information about the prospects for the particular R&D projects that the firm is undertaking. For example, investors devote considerable attention to analyst reports and news articles about the potential outcomes of clinical phase trials conducted by a biotech and pharmaceutical firm, while historical performance of past R&D efforts receives less media attention. According to Kahneman and Lovallo (1993, p. 17), people tend to consider the judgment or decision problem they are facing as unique and, in consequence, "neglect the statistics of the past in evaluating current plans." Kahneman and Lovallo call a focus on the uniqueness of the problem the "inside view" and a focus on relevant statistical performance data from previous trials the "outside view."

An excessive focus on the inside view implies that people will tend to be over- optimistic about prospects for success when they neglect unfavourable non-salient statistical information and tend to be less optimistic, and perhaps over-pessimistic, about the prospects of success, when they neglect favourable statistical information.

An alternative argument for why innovative efficiency would predict higher future returns derives from the q-theory (Cochrane, 1991, 1996; Liu, Whited, and Zhang, 2009). Firms with higher innovative efficiency tend to be more profitable and have higher return on assets. All else equal, the q-theory implies that higher profitability predicts higher returns because a high return on assets indicates that these assets were purchased by the firm at a discount (i.e., that they carry a high risk premium).

Specifically, suppose that the market for capital being purchased by a firm is competitive and efficient. When a firm makes an R&D expenditure to purchase innovative capital, the price it pays is appropriately discounted for risk. For concreteness, we can think, for example, of a firm that acquires a high-tech target at a competitive market price. In this scenario, a firm on average achieves higher return (large number of patents, resulting in high cash flows) on its innovative expenditures as fair compensation if its purchased innovative capital is highly risky, and it receives low return if capital is relatively low-risk. Past innovative efficiency is, therefore, a proxy for risk, so firms that have high past innovative efficiency (IE) should subsequently be productive in patenting (Dierickx and Cool, 1989) and earn higher profits and stock returns.4 In other words, q-theory also predicts a positive IE-return relation.

To test their key hypothesis that innovative efficiency is positively associated with contemporaneous stock market valuation and positively predicts future operating performance, market valuation, and stock returns, they use two measures of innovative efficiency in year t: patents granted in year t scaled by R&D capital in year t -2 (Patents/RDC) and adjusted patent citations received in year t by patents granted in years t-1 to t-5 scaled by the sum of R&D expenses in years t-3 to t-7 (Citations/ RD). The lag between the innovative input (R&D) and output (patents) reflects the average two-year application-grant lag. These IE measures are in general not highly correlated with other innovation-related return and operating performance predictors, such as R&D-to-market equity (Chan, Lakonishok, and Sougiannis, 2001), significant R&D growth (Eberhart, Maxwell, and Siddique, 2004), patents-to-market equity, and change in adjusted patent citations scaled by average total assets (Gu, 2005). There- fore, the IE measures potentially contain useful incremental information.

Fama-MacBeth (1973) regressions show that a higher IE measure (using a logarithmic transform of IE) predicts significantly higher return on assets (ROA) and cash flows (CF) over the next year after extensive controls. They also find that both current and lagged IE are significantly positively associated with equity market-to-book (MTB) using Fama-MacBeth regressions that control for abnormal earnings, R&D tax shields, R&D-to-book equity, RDG, PAT/ME, DAPC, AD/ME, CapEx/ME, and industry.

Furthermore, a significantly positive relation exists between the two IE measures and future stock returns using Fama-MacBeth regressions that control for various possible industry variables and return predictors, including RD/ME, RDG, PAT/ME, DAPC, size, book-to-market equity (BTM), momentum, CapEx/ME, AD/ME, ROA, asset growth, net stock issues, and institutional ownership. These findings support our hypotheses that innovative efficiency contains distinct information about future operating performance and market valuation that is incremental to that of other innovation measures and firm characteristics.

Portfolio analysis confirms the significantly positive relation between IE and future operating performance as well as stock returns. They sort firms with non-missing IE measures into three IE portfolios (Low, Middle, and High) based on the 33rd and 66th percentiles of the IE measures, and they find that the high IE groups in general have the highest ROA, cash flows, earnings, and profit margin averaged over the subsequent 5 years. The monthly value-weighted size-adjusted returns in excess of the one- month Treasury bill rate for the IE portfolios increase monotonically with IE: 49, 86, and 90 basis points for the low, middle, and high Patents/RDC portfolios, respectively, and 59, 81, and 85 basis points for the low, middle, and high Citations/RD portfolios, respectively.

Innovative efficiency and market valuation

Explanatory variable	Panel A: $IE = Patents/RDC$				Panel B: $IE = Citations/RD$			
$\ln(1+IE_{i,t})$	1.95	1.90	6.35	1.99	2.69	2.90	4.82	3.91
	(5.57)	(4.65)	(11.25)	(4.97)	(5.77)	(6.70)	(7.40)	(8.52)
$\ln(1+IE_{i,t-1})$		0.92		4.52		0.41		1.48
		(2.74)		(10.93)		(1.91)		(2.97)
$RDG_{i,t}$			-17.05	-11.86			-16.62	-11.72
			(-8.99)	(-6.32)			(-8.89)	(-6.31)
$\ln(1+PAT_{i,t}/ME_{i,t})$			-8.98	-7.04			-6.94	-5.66
			(-11.48)	(-18.68)			(-9.20)	(-14.32)
$\Delta APC_{i,t}$			1.30	1.07			0.89	0.83
			(3.79)	(4.31)			(2.71)	(3.43)
$RD_{i,t}/BE_{i,t}$	18.43	18.82	21.76	20.67	18.28	18.68	21.00	20.24
	(29.18)	(28.78)	(30.66)	(30.99)	(29.64)	(29.19)	(10.99)	(31.06)
$1/BE_{i,t}$	25.27	24.69	25.04	24.43	25.42	24.82	25.53	24.66
	(13.57)	(13.54)	(13.63)	(13.45)	(13.76)	(13.67)	(14.43)	(13.75)
Abnormal earnings$_{i,t}$	79.16	75.77	79.78	76.26	79.09	75.73	80.10	76.33
	(28.91)	(29.33)	(28.76)	(29.67)	(28.99)	(29.43)	(28.95)	(29.82)
RD tax shields$_{i,t}$	14.64	14.03	14.77	13.92	14.27	13.68	14.39	13.57
	(7.78)	(7.84)	(8.22)	(8.26)	(7.80)	(7.87)	(8.20)	(8.22)
$\ln(1+AD_{i,t}/ME_{i,t})$	-5.80	-4.58	-5.38	-4.22	-5.74	-4.52	-5.34	-4.18
	(-8.44)	(-7.04)	(-7.49)	(-6.36)	(-8.33)	(-6.89)	(-7.18)	(-6.12)
$\ln(1+CapEx_{i,t}/ME_{i,t})$	-20.94	-17.14	-19.43	-15.89	-20.87	-17.08	-19.76	-15.99
	(-23.19)	(-28.75)	(-22.37)	(-25.74)	(-23.56)	(-29.62)	(-22.91)	(-26.67)
Intercept	-34.43	-36.71	-33.10	-36.04	-34.49	-36.76	-33.04	-36.09
	(-5.90)	(-5.94)	(-5.31)	(-5.81)	(-5.49)	(-5.94)	(-5.31)	(-5.82)
Industry dummy	Yes	Yes	Yes	Yes	Yes	Yes	Yes	Yes
Adjusted R^2	75.51	74.15	76.15	74.10	75.55	73.81	76.09	74.14

This table reports the average slopes (in percent) and their time series t-statistics in parentheses from annual Fama-MacBeth (1973) cross-sectional regressions of the natural log of firms' market-to-book equity (MTB) ratio in year t on innovative efficiency (IE) in year t and year t-1 and other control variables in year t. The subscript i denotes firm i. ln(1þIE) is the natural log of Patents/RDC or Citations/RD (both defined in Table 1). RDG is a dummy for significant R&D growth. ln(1þPAT/ME) denotes the natural log of one plus patent counts divided by year-end market equity. DAPC is change in adjusted patent citations scaled by average total assets (defined in Table 2). RD/BE denotes R&D expenditure divided by book value of equity.

Abnormal earnings are earnings after extraordinary items before expensing R&D expenses and less preferred dividends for firm i in year t, ti,t is tax rate (total tax expenses divided by pretax book income) for firm i in year t, and rt is the one-year Treasury bill rate in year t. R&D tax shields denotes R&D expenditure multiplied by tax rate, scaled by book value of equity. ln(1þAD/ME) is the natural log of one plus annual advertising expenditure divided by year-end market equity. ln(1þCapEx/ME) is the natural log of one plus annual capital expenditure divided by year-end market equity, and Industry dummies are based on the Fama and French (1997) 48 industries. They winsorize all variables at the 1% and 99% levels and standardize all independent variables to zero mean and 1 standard deviation. The reported adjusted R2 is the time series average of the adjusted R2 of each annual cross-sectional regression.

The risk-adjusted returns of the IE portfolios also increase monotonically with IE. Specifically, the monthly value-weighted alphas estimated from the Carhart (1997) four-factor model for the low, middle, and high Patents/ RDC portfolios are -19, 22, and 27 basis points, respectively, and the monthly Carhart alphas for the low, middle, and high Citations/RD portfolios are - 9, 14, and 26 basis points, respectively. Furthermore, the positive alphas of the high IE portfolios are statistically significant at the 1% level, which indicates that high IE firms are undervalued relative to the Carhart model benchmark. In unreported results, they find the difference in the Carhart alphas between the high and low IE portfolios is also statistically significant at the 1% level for both IE measures.

Innovative efficiency (IE) portfolio returns and risk factor models

	Excess return (percent)	Carhart four-factor model					Investment-based three-factor model			
IE		α (percent)	*MKT*	*SMB*	*HML*	*MOM*	α (percent)	*MKT*	*INV*	*ROE*
Panel A: *Patents/RDC*										
Low	0.49	−0.19	1.08	0.57	−0.14	−0.05	0.10	1.10	−0.13	−0.37
t	(1.48)	(−2.20)	(45.31)	(16.47)	(−3.22)	(−1.70)	(0.74)	(31.74)	(−1.89)	(−6.74)
Middle	0.86	0.22	1.01	0.49	−0.18	−0.02	0.39	1.07	−0.00	−0.29
t	(2.78)	(2.48)	(43.89)	(10.42)	(−3.67)	(−0.61)	(2.40)	(30.98)	(−0.05)	(−3.80)
High	0.90	0.27	1.04	0.53	−0.21	−0.04	0.50	1.08	−0.04	−0.37
t	(2.79)	(3.08)	(41.96)	(10.79)	(−5.80)	(−1.35)	(3.08)	(31.25)	(−0.63)	(−5.22)
Panel B: *Citations/RD*										
Low	0.59	−0.09	1.05	0.55	−0.13	−0.03	0.17	1.08	−0.07	−0.33
t	(1.86)	(−0.94)	(40.67)	(13.72)	(−2.94)	(−0.95)	(1.15)	(30.00)	(−1.04)	(−5.33)
Middle	0.81	0.14	1.01	0.44	−0.06	−0.03	0.25	1.05	0.08	−0.21
t	(2.78)	(1.65)	(49.27)	(13.02)	(−1.44)	(−1.00)	(1.85)	(31.16)	(1.20)	(−3.60)
High	0.85	0.26	1.04	0.49	−0.26	−0.05	0.49	1.08	−0.11	−0.38
t	(2.65)	(3.07)	(41.67)	(10.34)	(−7.23)	(−1.68)	(3.15)	(33.73)	(−1.69)	(−5.62)

At the end of June of year t from 1982 to 2007, they sort firms independently into two size groups (small "S" or big "B") based on the NYSE median size breakpoint at the end of June of year t and three IE groups (low "L," middle "M," or high "H") based on the 33rd and 66th percentiles of IE in year t-1. They measure IE by Patents/RDC and Citations/RD in Panels A and B, respectively. They hold these portfolios over the next 12 months and compute value-weighted monthly returns of these size-IE portfolios (S/H, B/H, S/M, B/M, S/L, and B/L). They then calculate monthly size-adjusted returns of the low, middle, and high IE portfolios as (S/LþB/L)/2, (S/MþB/M)/2, and (S/HþB/H)/2, respectively. This table reports the monthly average size-adjusted excess returns to these portfolios and the intercepts (a, in percentage) and risk factor loadings from regressing portfolio excess returns on factor returns. Heteroskedasticity-robust t-statistics are reported in parentheses. Excess return is the difference between size-adjusted portfolio returns and the one- month Treasury bill rate. MKT, SMB, and HML are the market, size, and book-to-market ratio factors of Fama and French (1993). MOM is the momentum factor of Carhart (1997). INV and ROE are the investment and profitability factors from Chen, Novy-Marx, and Zhang (2011).

These patterns are similar for alphas estimated from the Fama and French (1993) three-factor model and the investment-based three-factor model (Chen, Novy-Marx, and Zhang, 2011). In addition, the high IE portfolio generally has lower loadings than the low IE portfolio on the market factor, suggesting that high IE firms are less risky than low IE firms.

To examine whether the financing-based mispricing factor Undervalued Minus Overvalued (UMO; Hirshleifer and Jiang, 2010) helps explain the IE effect, they add UMO to the Carhart model and the investment-based model. They find the alphas estimated from these augmented models for the high IE portfolios remain significantly positive at the 1% level. This evidence indicates that the IE effect is incremental to the mispricing effect as captured by UMO. In addition, the alphas estimated from these augmented models increase monotonically with IE. In unreported results, they find the difference in the alphas estimated from these two augmented models between the high and low IE portfolios is also statistically significant at the 1% level for both IE measures.

If the IE-return relation represents a market inefficiency driven by psychological constraints such as limited attention, they expect to observe greater return predictability among stocks with low investor attention and among hard-to-value stocks. To test this hypothesis, they use size and analyst coverage as proxies for attention to a stock (Hong, Lim, and Stein, 2000) and firm age, turnover, and idiosyncratic volatility as proxies for valuation uncertainty (Kumar, 2009). They expect a stronger IE effect among firms with small market capitalization, low analyst coverage (AC), young age, high turnover, and high idiosyncratic volatility (IVOL).

The Fama-MacBeth subsample regressions provide supporting evidence. The average IE slopes among low attention and hard-to-value stocks are in general statistically significant and are substantially larger than those among high attention and easy-to-value stocks, which often are insignificant. For example, the slope on Citations/RD is 0.08% (t ¼ 2.21) in low AC firms, but only 0.05% (t ¼

1.65) in high AC firms. Similarly, the slope on Citations/RD is 0.11% (t 1⁄4 3.26) in young firms, but only 0.02% (t 1⁄4 0.91) in old firms. In addition, the slope on Citations/RD is 0.08% (t1⁄42.08) in high IVOL firms, but only 0.03% (t1⁄41.34) in low IVOL firms. Although the cross- subsample differences in the IE slopes are not always statistically significant, their magnitudes are economically substantial.

To further examine if the IE-based return predictability is driven by risk, mispricing, or both, they construct a factor-mimicking portfolio for innovative efficiency, Efficient Minus Inefficient (EMI), based on Patents/RDC (EMI1) and on Citations/RD (EMI2) following the procedure in Fama and French (1993). Specifically, at the end of June of year t from 1982 to 2007, they sort firms independently into two size groups (small "S" or big "B") based on the NYSE median size breakpoint at the end of June of year t, and three IE groups (low "L," middle "M," or high "H") based on the 33rd and 66th percentiles of IE in year t-1. The intersection of these portfolios forms six size-IE portfolios (S/L, S/M, S/H, B/L, B/M, and B/H). Value-weighted monthly returns on these six portfolios are computed from July of year t to June of year tþ1. The EMI factor is computed as (S/HþB/H)/2-(S/LþB/L)/2.

They find that these two EMI factors are not highly correlated with well-known factors such as the market, size, value and momentum factors (Carhart 1997), the investment and return on equity (ROE) factors (Chen, Novy-Marx, and Zhang, 2011), and the UMO factor

(Hirshleifer and Jiang, 2010). The correlations between the EMI factors and these well-known factors range from –0.15 to 0.13.

In addition, they construct four innovation-related factors based on RD/ME, RDG, PAT/ME, and DAPC, following the same method in constructing the EMI factors. They find that the EMI factors are not highly correlated with these four factors, except for the PAT/ME factor. The correlations between the EMI factors and the RD/ME, RDG, and DAPC factors range from 0.07 to 0.36. The correlation with the PAT/ME factor is 0.66 for EMI1 and 0.52 for EMI2.

The average monthly return of the EMI1 factor is 0.41%, which is higher than that of the size factor (0.07%), the value factor (0.37%), the investment factor (0.36%), the RDG factor (0.21%), the PAT/ME factor (0.31%), and the DAPC factor (0.00%). Furthermore, EMI1 offers an ex post Sharpe ratio, 0.23, which is higher than that of all the above factors except the mispricing factor (0.27). The EMI2 factor has similar but slightly lower average monthly return (0.26%) and ex post Sharpe ratio (0.15). The high level of the equity premium is a well-known puzzle for rational asset pricing theory (Mehra and Prescott, 1985). Therefore, on the face of it, the high ex post Sharpe ratios associated with the EMI factors also suggest that the IE-return relation can be too strong to be entirely explained by rational risk premium.

Adding EMI1 to the Fama and French three factors increases the ex post Sharpe ratio of the tangency portfolio from 0.29 to 0.39

with a weight of 42% on EMI1. Even when all of the above factors are included, the weight on EMI1 in the tangency portfolio is 22%, which is substantially higher than that of any of the other factors. Adding EMI2 to the Fama and French three factors increases the ex post Sharpe ratio of the tangency portfolio from 0.29 to 0.34 with a weight of 33% on EMI2. Even when all of the above factors are included, the weight on EMI2 in the tangency portfolio is 15.65%, which is higher than that of any of the other factors except the mispricing factor (17.22%) and the market factor (16.00%). These findings imply the IE-return relation captures return predictability effects above and beyond those captured by the other well-known factors and the four innovation-related factors they construct.

Efficient Minus Inefficient (EMI) factors and market factor returns over time

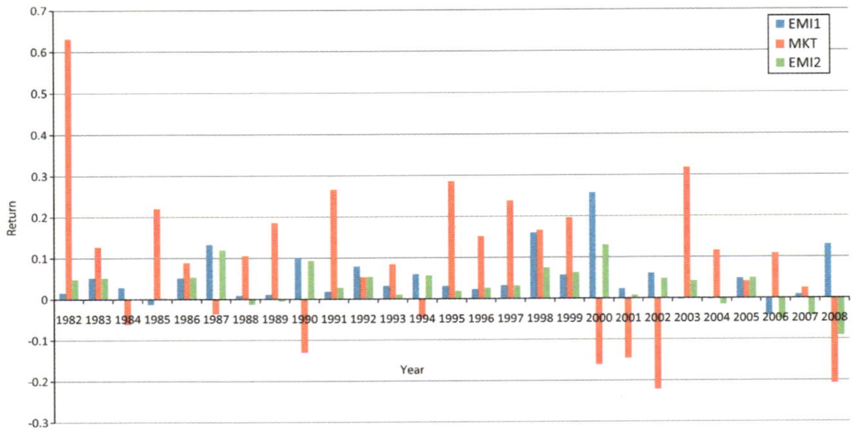

This figure plots the return (on a per annum basis) for the EMI1 and EMI2 factors and the market factor from 1982 to 2008. MKT is the return on the value-weighted NYSE, Amex, and Nasdaq portfolio minus the one-month Treasury bill rate. At the end of June of year t from 1982 to 2007, we sort firms independently into two size groups (small "S" or big "B") based on the NYSE median size breakpoint and three innovative efficiency (IE) groups (low "L," middle "M," or high "H") based on the 33rd and 66th percentiles of our IE measures, Patents/RDC and Citations/RD in year t-1. Size is the market equity at the end of June of year t. The intersection of these portfolios forms six size–IE portfolios (S/L, S/M, S/H, B/L, B/M, and B/H). Value-weighted monthly returns on these six double-sorted portfolios in excess of the one-month Treasury bill rate are computed from July of year t to June of year tþ1. EMI1 (EMI2) is computed as (S/HþB/H)/2 (S/LþB/L)/2, where "H" and "L" refer to IE portfolios based on Patents/RDC (Citations/RD).

Their study offers a new innovation-related measure, IE, which is contemporaneously associated with market valuation and predicts future operating performance and stock returns. Existing studies relating to innovation and the stock market focus on the effects of either the input (R&D) or the output (patents) of innovation separately. Their paper differs in focusing on innovative efficiency as a ratio of innovative output to input, based on the idea that efficiency should be highly value-relevant. They find that the predictive power of innovative efficiency is incremental to that of other innovation-related variables such as R&D intensity, significant R&D growth, patent counts, and citations. They also examine whether the IE effect is driven by risk or mispricing, and they explore how the IE effect interacts with proxies for limited attention and valuation uncertainty.

3. MEASURING IP IMPACT

To test our key hypothesis that AI-IP is positively associated with contemporaneous stock market valuation and positively predicts future operating performance, market valuation and stock returns, we first measure the current impact of a company's AI-IP compared to the other companies in its industry:

3.1 CURRENT IMPACT INDEX (CII)

The idea of a patent is simple. An inventor or his/her company is granted a 20-year monopoly on an invention, in return for detailed disclosure of how the invention works. Rather than stifle innovation, the idea is that patents should spur innovation. Through the patent system, inventors get 20 years of exclusive control of their inventions, while the public is able to see how the current inventions work and can, therefore, build and improve upon them without the pitfalls of starting from scratch.

When an inventor applies for a patent, he must show that the invention is novel, useful, and non-obvious to someone with average expertise in the same industry. To achieve this, the inventor will cite earlier patents and explain why the new patent improves on the earlier inventions. The patent examiner may also add earlier inventions that limit the scope of the new invention. A U.S. patent typically cites seven or eight earlier patents in the "references cited" section of its front page. These references cited – also called "backward citations" – in essence, identify the important prior art that has contributed to or limits the claims of the just-issued patent.

The fundamental idea of patent citation analysis is that when a patent is highly cited (by many later patents), it is likely to contain important technological advances upon which many subsequent developments have built. In other words, highly cited patents are regarded as markers for important new ideas, identifying quality assets in a company's patent portfolio. A number of previous studies have provided support for this assumption. Carpenter et al. found that patents related to IR 100 invention awards are cited twice as often as typical patents. Similarly, Breitzman and Narin showed patents assigned Pioneering Patent status were cited much more often than average, as were patents accorded Hall of Fame status by the U.S.

Patent & Trademark Office (USPTO). In another study, Albert et al. in cooperation with Eastman Kodak Laboratories reported that patents Kodak's staff saw as important were more frequently cited than patents they regarded as less important.

There is also evidence to suggest that patent citations may have some validity as a proxy for patents' commercial value. A study by Harhoff et al. showed that patents regarded as commercially valuable by their owners are more highly cited than patents regarded as less valuable. In addition, a study by Thomas revealed that highly cited patents are more likely to be renewed than patents that receive fewer citations (U.S. patents must be renewed 4, 8 and 12 years after their issue date). Given that patent assignees must pay renewal fees at each of the three renewal points, the decision to renew patents is an economic one. Patent assignees will only renew patents if they expect the commercial returns on those patents to exceed their renewal fee. The finding that highly cited patents are more likely to be renewed therefore suggests that patent assignees expect higher commercial returns from these patents.

The Current Impact Index (CII) is calculated with the mean value of all forward citations of identified AI-IP publications of a company, published within the previous 365 days, scaled by the mean value of all forward citations of identified AI-IP publications of all companies from the same industry, published within the previous 365 days. This measure expresses the technological impact of a company's AI-IP compared to its industry peers. For example, a value of

1.10 would mean that the company's current AI-IP impact is 10% higher than its peers at the day of the calculation.

Ordinary least squares (OLS) regression show that the CII correlates highly with future stock returns, with different lag times per industry. This is expected, as the industries in general show different innovation characteristics and speed:

Results

Industry	CII OLS lag (mean)	Lowest_p (mean)
Television Services	7.00	0.00
Integrated oil Companies	9.00	0.00
Other Consumer Services	25.00	0.00
Construction/Ag Equipment/Trucks	17.00	0.00
Major Chemicals	19.56	0.01
Building Products	16.00	0.01
Medical Specialities	20.25	0.01
Telecommunications Equipment	9.27	0.02
Computer Communications Equipment	16.50	0.02

Multi-Sector Companies	3.00	0.02
Oilfield Services/Equipment	17.00	0.03
Industrial Machinery/Components	13.33	0.03
Medical/Dental Instruments	14.23	0.04
Electronic Components	12.62	0.04
EDP Services	17.65	0.04
Biotechnology: Electromedical & Electrotherapeutic Apparatus	22.99	0.04
Office Equipment/Supplies/Services	23.60	0.04
Catalog/Specialty Distribution	24.00	0.05
Industrial Specialties	8.47	0.05
Biotechnology: In Vitro & In Vivo Diagnostic Substances	17.59	0.06
Aerospace	12.50	0.06
Consumer Electronics/Appliances	9.71	0.07
Biotechnology: Laboratory Analytical Instruments	20.25	0.07
Computer Software: Prepackaged Software	15.91	0.08

Computer Manufacturing	14.22	0.09
Major Pharmaceuticals	15.52	0.09
Semiconductors	16.76	0.09
Business Services	8.59	0.10
Computer peripheral equipment	13.55	0.11
Biotechnology: Biological Products (No Diagnostic Substances)	24.35	0.12
Radio And Television Broadcasting And Communications Equipment	26.43	0.13
Computer Software: Programm-ing, Data Processing	17.10	0.14
Electric Utilities: Central	29.00	0.35

OLS regression between logarithmic adjusted close prices (as depending variable) and forward lagged CII (t+1 to t+30) on a monthly basis. The p-value for each term tests the null hypothesis that the coefficient is equal to zero (no effect). A low p-value (< 0.10) indicates that the null hypothesis can be rejected. In other words, a predictor that has a low p-value is likely to be a meaningful addition to a model because changes in the predictor‘s value are related to changes in the response variable. Conversely, a larger (insignificant) p-value suggests that changes in the predictor are not associated with changes in the response. In the table above, we can see that the lagged correlations for almost all of the industries are significant. The table above also shows the average lag-time in months for each industry with the highest OLS regression p-value. For example, high tech companies tend to turn IP into revenues much faster than f.e. Electric Utility companies. The average lag times in the table above confirm this theory.

Example: NVIDIA Corporation (NVDA)

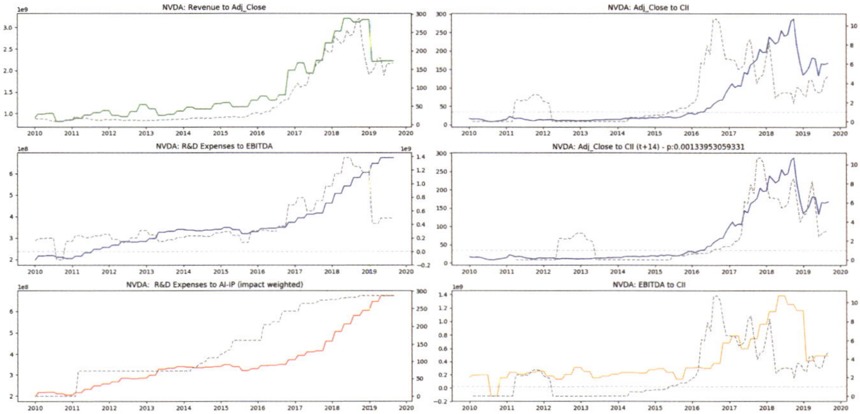

The plots above show: (i) The company's revenue versus its stock price (on an adjusted base not considering stock splits, etc.); (ii) The company's R&D expenses versus its EBITDA; (iii) The company's R&D expenses versus its accumulated AI-IP; (iv) The company's stock price versus its CII; (v) The company's stock price versus its forward lagged CII; (vi) The company's EBITDA versus its CII.

Example: Dare Bioscience, Inc. (DARE)

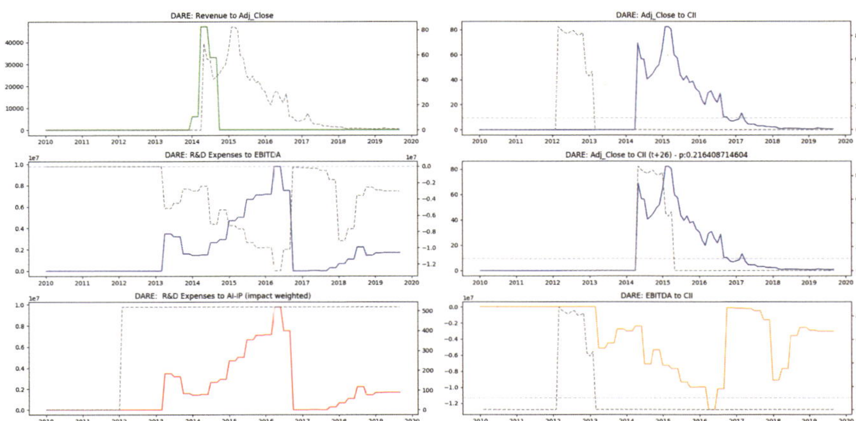

The plots above show: (i) The company's revenue versus its stock price (on an adjusted base not considering stock splits, etc.); (ii) The company's R&D expenses versus its EBITDA; (iii) The company's R&D expenses versus its accumulated AI-IP; (iv) The company's stock price versus its CII; (v) The company's stock price versus its forward lagged CII; (vi) The company's EBITDA versus its CII.

Example: Endurance International Group H (EIGI)

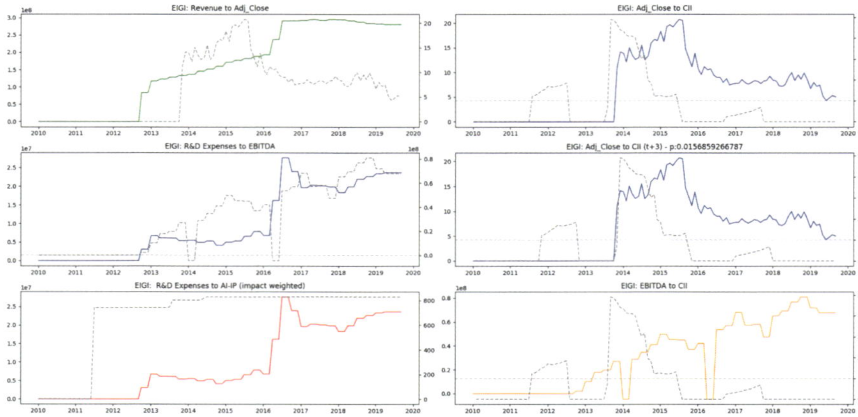

The plots above show: (i) The company's revenue versus its stock price (on an adjusted base not considering stock splits, etc.); (ii) The company's R&D expenses versus its EBITDA; (iii) The company's R&D expenses versus its accumulated AI-IP; (iv) The company's stock price versus its CII; (v) The company's stock price versus its forward lagged CII; (vi) The company's EBITDA versus its CII.

Example: Impinj, Inc. (PI)

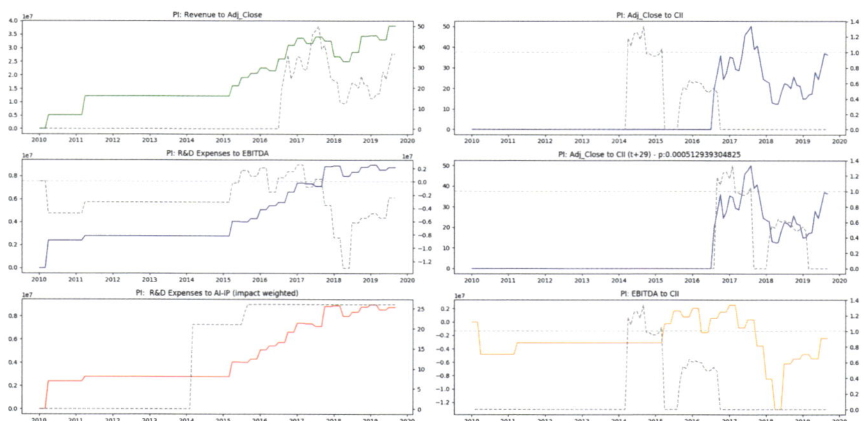

The plots above show: (i) The company's revenue versus its stock price (on an adjusted base not considering stock splits, etc.); (ii) The company's R&D expenses versus its EBITDA; (iii) The company's R&D expenses versus its accumulated AI-IP; (iv) The company's stock price versus its CII; (v) The company's stock price versus its forward lagged CII; (vi) The company's EBITDA versus its CII.

Example: Dicerna Pharmaceuticals, Inc. (DRNA)

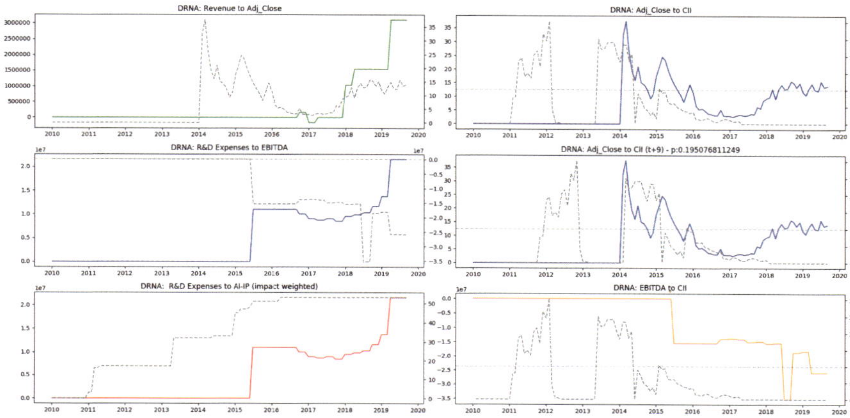

The plots above show: (i) The company's revenue versus its stock price (on an adjusted base not considering stock splits, etc.); (ii) The company's R&D expenses versus its EBITDA; (iii) The company's R&D expenses versus its accumulated AI-IP; (iv) The company's stock price versus its CII; (v) The company's stock price versus its forward lagged CII; (vi) The company's EBITDA versus its CII.

4. FORECASTING IP BASED FAIR MARKET VALUE

To finally test our key hypothesis that AI-IP is positively associated with contemporaneous stock market valuation and positively predicts future operating performance, market valuation and stock returns, we create a model to forecast its AI-IP to market value on a monthly basis:

4.1. AI-IP TO MARKET VALUE INDICATOR (IPI)

Modeling time varying data is a fundamental problem in Data Science with applications in a variety of fields such as medicine, finance, economics, meteorology, and customer support center operations. Using models trained on time series data to forecast future values is a well studied area to which methods ranging from classical statistical models such as Autoregressive integrated moving average (ARIMA), simple machine learning techniques such as support vector machines (SVM) have been applied. Of recent interest is the application of recurrent neural network (RNN), particularly networks based on state-of-the-art Long short-term memory (LSTMs) cells. LSTM-based methods have shown great success in short-horizon forecasting, where forecasts are made for a small number of timesteps beyond the last observations recorded in training data. Examples of this short horizon forecasts are stock prediction, recommender systems and ICU diagnosis.

To create a robust AI-IP to market value model, we incorporate multiple parameters like R&D expenses, AI-IP, CII or revenue into the model. In this book we are applying a Long Short-Term Memory (LSTM) recurrent neural network. We frame the supervised learning problem as predicting the stock prices at the current month (t) given the CII values at the prior 24 time steps (2 years), the R&D expenses at the prior 4 time steps and the revenues at the prior 4 time steps (4 months). As the OLS regression above showed, lag times for up to 2 years before can be an important measurement. The input values have been normalized and chosen because of the evidently strong correlation between R&D expenses, intellectual property and resulting revenues.

For each of the companies, a dedicated Long Short-Term Memory

(LSTM) recurrent neural network is being trained over 50 epochs. We define the LSTM with 50 neurons in the first hidden layer and 1 neuron in the output layer for predicting stock values. The input shape consists of 32 features (24 CII + 4 R&D + 4 revenue). We are using the Mean Absolute Error (MAE) loss function and the efficient Adam version of stochastic gradient descent.

Results

Industry	IPI Correlation (mean)
Catalog/Specialty Distribution	0.98
Consumer Electronics/Video Chains	0.95
Television Services	0.92
Electric Utilities: Central	0.90
Medical Electronics	0.89
Industrial Specialties	0.86
Biotechnology: Electromedical & Electrotherapeutic Apparatus	0.84
Biotechnology: Commercial Physical & Biological Resarch	0.83
Plastic Products	0.81
Computer Software: Programming, Data Processing	0.80
Paints/Coatings	0.78
Semiconductors	0.78

Computer Software: Prepackaged Software	0.74
Major Pharmaceuticals	0.74
Business Services	0.74
Medical/Dental Instruments	0.73
Computer Manufacturing	0.73
Biotechnology: Biological Pro-ucts (No Diagnostic Substances)	0.72
Oilfield Services/Equipment	0.72
Biotechnology: Laboratory Analytical Instruments	0.70
Major Chemicals	0.69
Multi-Sector Companies	0.69
Aerospace	0.68
EDP Services	0.68
Agricultural Chemicals	0.67
Consumer Electronics/Appliances	0.65
Computer peripheral equipment	0.63
Electronic Components	0.57
Biotechnology: In Vitro & In Vivo Diagnostic Substances	0.56
Medical Specialities	0.53

The correlation coefficient r measures the strength and direction of a linear relationship between two variables. The table above shows the average correlation coefficient r for each industry. A coefficient of 0.30 means a weak uphill (positive) linear relationship, 0.50 a moderate uphill (positive) relationship, 0.70 a strong uphill (positive) linear relationship and exactly 1 a perfect uphill (positive) linear relationship. The table above shows a significant correlation between the IPI and time lagged (t+1) stock price in most of the industries.

Example: NVIDIA Corporation (NVDA)

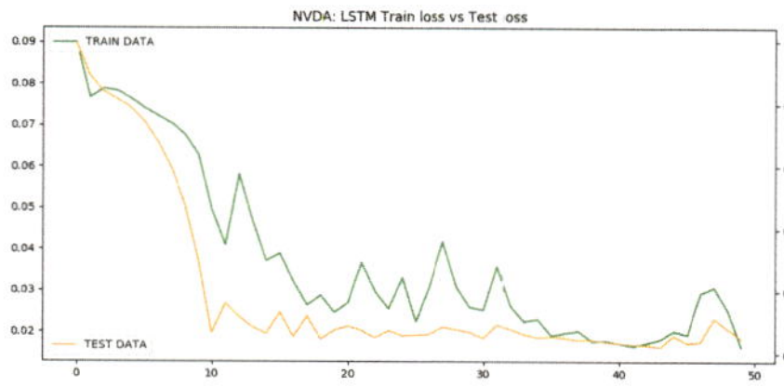

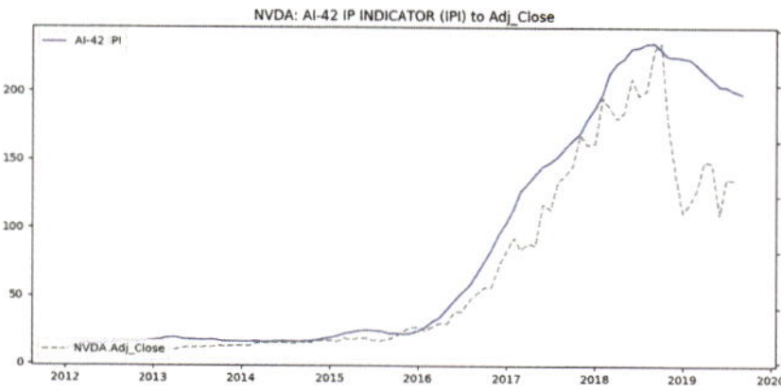

The plots above show: (i) The Mean Absolute Error (MAE) loss on the training and test data of the Long Short-Term Memory (LSTM) recurrent neural network; (ii) the IPI versus its stock price (on an adjusted base not considering stock splits, etc.)

Example: Alphabet Inc. (GOOG)

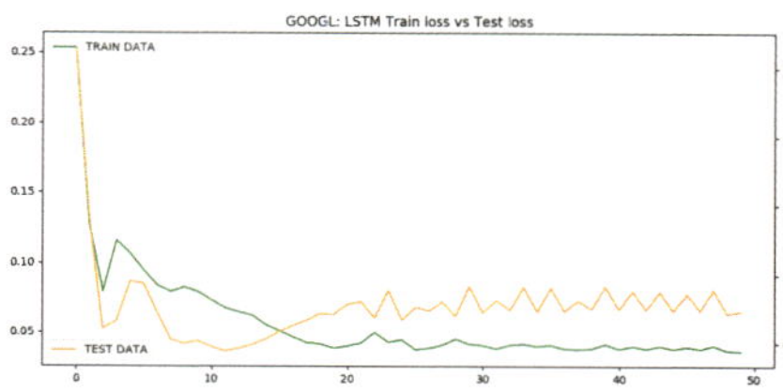

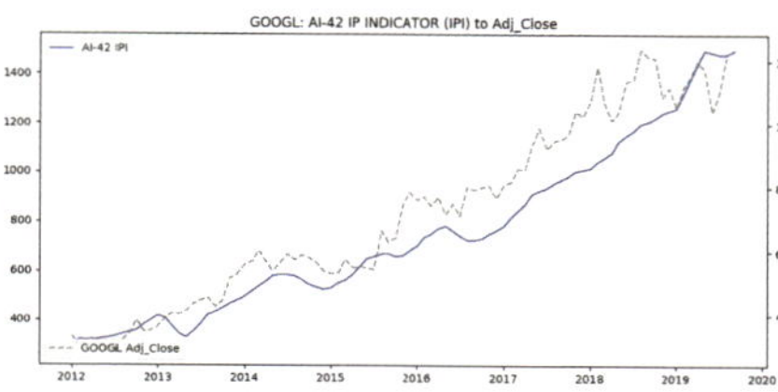

The plots above show: (i) The Mean Absolute Error (MAE) loss on the training and test data of the Long Short-Term Memory (LSTM) recurrent neural network; (ii) the IPI versus its stock price (on an adjusted base not considering stock splits, etc.)

Example: Apple, Inc. (AAPL)

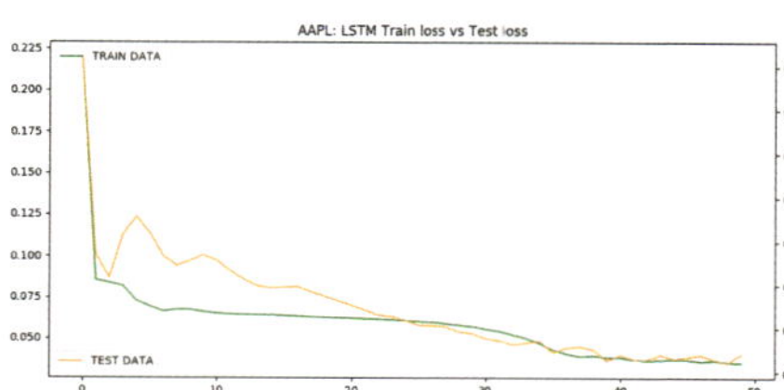

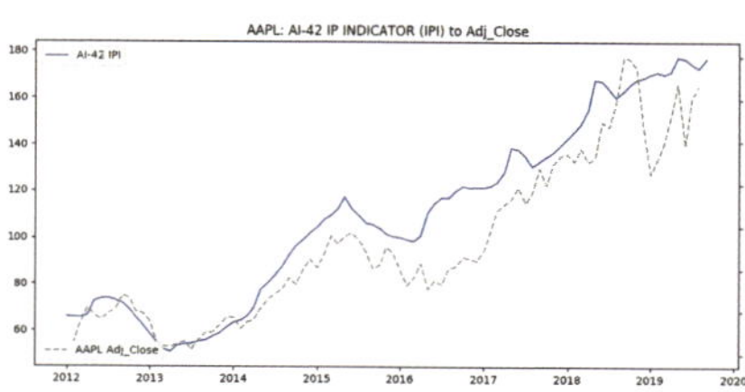

The plots above show: (i) The Mean Absolute Error (MAE) loss on the training and test data of the Long Short-Term Memory (LSTM) recurrent neural network; (ii) the IPI versus its stock price (on an adjusted base not considering stock splits, etc.)

Example: International Business Machines (IBM)

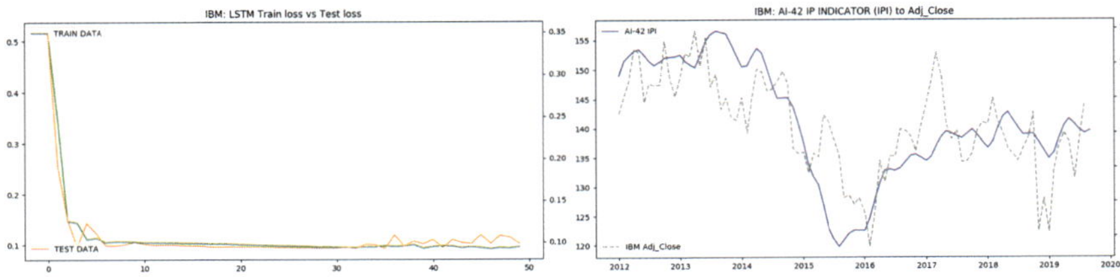

The plots above show: (i) The Mean Absolute Error (MAE) loss on the training and test data of the Long Short-Term Memory (LSTM) recurrent neural network; (ii) the IPI versus its stock price (on an adjusted base not considering stock splits, etc.)

Example: Microsoft Corporation (MSFT)

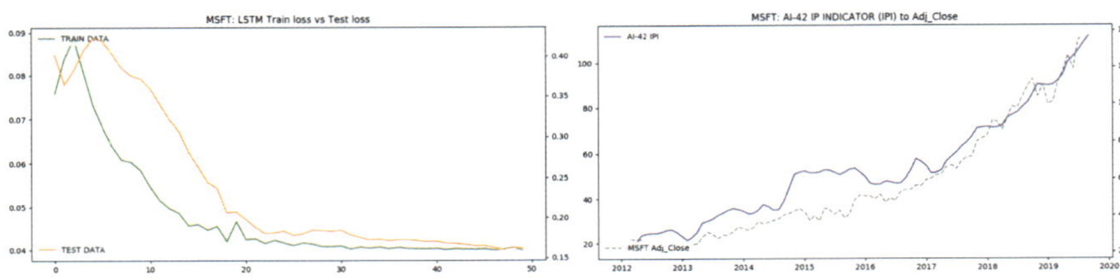

The plots above show: (i) The Mean Absolute Error (MAE) loss on the training and test data of the Long Short-Term Memory (LSTM) recurrent neural network; (ii) the IPI versus its stock price (on an adjusted base not considering stock splits, etc.)

Example: Xencor, Inc. (XNCR)

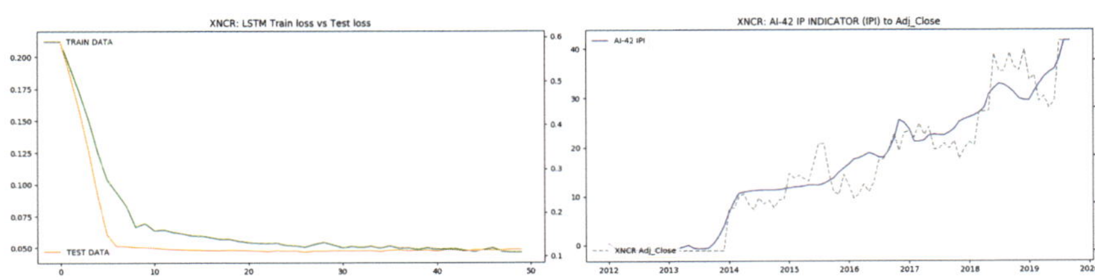

The plots above show: (i) The Mean Absolute Error (MAE) loss on the training and test data of the Long Short-Term Memory (LSTM) recurrent neural network; (ii) the IPI versus its stock price (on an adjusted base not considering stock splits, etc.)

A significantly positive relation exists between stock returns and the AI-IP to Market Value Indicator (IPI). This finding supports our hypotheses that AI-IP, its impact and related R&D expenses contain distinct information about future operating performance and market valuation that is incremental to that of other innovation measures and firm characteristics.

If the IPI-return relation represents a market inefficiency, we expect to observe greater returns when investing in companies with higher IPI predictions.

5. PORTFOLIO ANALYSIS

Portfolio analysis confirms the significantly positive relation between IPI and future stock returns. We sort firms with non-missing IPI measures into three portfolios: Panel A (all companies), Panel B (the top 25 companies, ranked by predicted IPI growth and indicator strength at each portfolio rebalancing date) and Panel C (the worst 25 companies, ranked by predicted IPI growth and indicator strength at each portfolio rebalancing date). We then simulate three portfolios for each panel, starting from January 1st 2017 up until July 1st 2019. At the first trading day of each quarter, we rebalance the portfolios accordingly. No trading costs are assumed as we want to compare the three panels directly.

Example: International Business Machines (IBM)

Date	Profit (%)	PuL (%)
2017-04-03	0.12	1.12
2017-07-03	0.07	1.20
2017-10-02	0.06	1.26
2018-01-02	0.04	1.31
2018-04-02	0.02	1.34
2018-07-02	0.14	1.53
2018-10-01	0.08	1.65
2019-01-02	-0.18	1.35
2019-04-01	0.30	1.77
2019-07-01	0.01	1.78

The table above shows: (i) The quarterly profit of the companies and (ii) the accumulated profit.

Results: Panel B (top companies)

Date	Profit	PuL
2017-04-03	0.10	1.10
2017-07-03	0.13	1.24
2017-10-02	0.16	1.44

2018-01-02	0.16	1.67
2018-04-02	0.10	1.84
2018-07-02	0.19	2.18
2018-10-01	0.28	2.80
2019-01-02	-0.21	2.22
2019-04-01	0.34	2.97
2019-07-01	0.14	3.37

The table above shows: (i) The quarterly profit of the companies and (ii) the accumulated profit.w

Example: International Business Machines (IBM)

Date	Profit	PuL
2017-04-03	0.02	1.02
2017-07-03	0.00	1.02
2017-10-02	0.06	1.09
2018-01-02	-0.07	1.02
2018-04-02	0.03	1.05
2018-07-02	0.21	1.27

2018-10-01	0.17	1.49
2019-01-02	-0.11	1.32
2019-04-01	0.28	1.69
2019-07-01	-0.08	1.55

The table above shows: (i) The quarterly profit of the companies and (ii) the accumulated profit.

This confirms our hypothesis. Panel A, all companies, generated an accumulated profit of +78%, which is representing the baseline. Panel C, the bad companies, could only generate +55% (-23% to baseline), significantly less than the baseline. Panel B, the top companies, generated a return of 237% (+159% to baseline), significantly more than the baseline.

Results: Comparison of Panel A, B and C

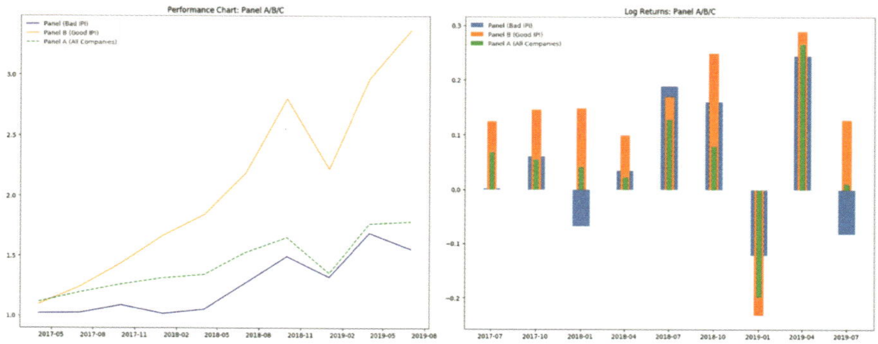

The book offers a new innovation-related measure, IPI, which is contemporaneously associated with market valuation and predicts future operating performance and stock returns. Existing studies relating to innovation and market performance focus on the effects of either the input (R&D) or the output (patents) of innovation separately. Our study differs in focusing on Artificial Intelligence based innovative efficiency as a ratio of innovative output to input, based on the idea that efficiency should be highly value relevant. We find that the predictive power of AI innovation is incremental to that of other innovation-related variables such as R&D intensity, significant R&D growth, patent counts and citations.

6. SUMMING-UP

In this book we demonstrate that analysing intangible assets of a company in great detail allows building a model to accurately forecast a company's ability to convert its intellectual property into stock value in the following quarter. We also demonstrate that a company's AI-IP impact correlates significantly with its future stock returns.

Our book offers a new IP-related measure, IPI, which is contemporaneously associated with market valuation and predicts future operating performance and stock returns. Existing studies relating to innovation and market performance focus on the effects of either the input (R&D) or the output (patents) of innovation separately. Our study differs in focusing on Artificial Intelligence based innovative efficiency as a ratio of innovative output to input, based on the idea that efficiency should be highly value relevant. We find that the predictive power of AI innovation is incremental to that of other innovation related variables such as R&D intensity, significant R&D growth, patent counts and citations.

It can be shown that lagged correlations of the introduced CII (Current Impact Index) for almost all of the industries are significant, as well as the correlation between the introduced IPI (AI-IP to Market Value Indicator) and the time lagged (t+1) stock price is significant in most of the industries.

We find that a long only portfolio strategy that takes advantage of the indicators presented in this book yields abnormal positive returns that portfolio analysis confirms our hypothesis and show that a portfolio of top companies generated a return of 237% (+159% to baseline), which is significantly higher than the market (+78%).

Our findings suggest that it is possible to identify potential winners and losers based on IP related information and that such information can add additional value to every asset management strategy.

7. THE AI-42 INDEX™

The findings discussed above are also leading to other interesting use-cases. For example, these can be used for the construction of industry indices or for the selection of index constituents and weightings.

The Dow Jones Industrial Average (DJIA) is a stock market index that shows how 30 large, publicly owned companies based in the United States have traded during a standard trading session in the stock market. It is one of the most important financial indicators worldwide. Consequently, and given the rise of Artificial Intelligence, 42.cx has introduced the AI-42 INDEX™ for publicly traded companies. The AI-42 INDEX™ is an alpha weighted market index based on the market opportunities of the 42 greatest Artificial Intelligence public companies.

The index weighting is determined by a proprietary formula based on analytics and expert rankings. It was constructed as of January 1st 2017 and is rebalanced quarterly. Out of the top AI-IP rated global artificial intelligence companies, the most influential companies are being selected by a scientific and strategic board by assessing the disruptive and strategic potential, the underlying AI technology, perceived risk and expected returns on the basis of a weighting of several characteristics of the prospective company.

It seems that the index is appropriately showing the growth of the Artificial Intelligence asset class. The chart below shows the historical development of the index since its interception in 2017, where it started at 4.692,77 points and grew since then to 10,376.94 points (+121%) over a period of a little more than two years:

AI-42 INDEX™

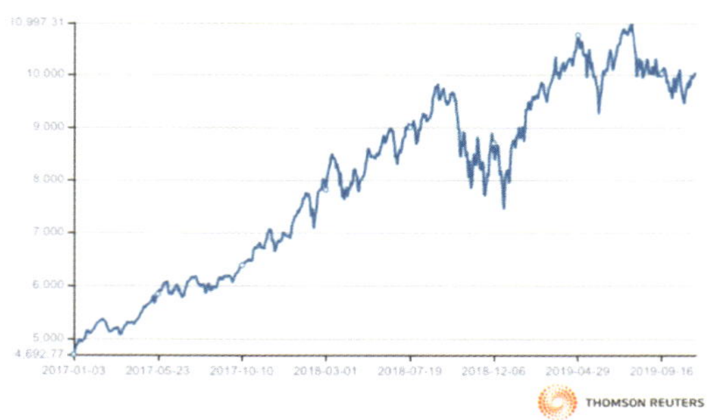

The current and historical prices of the AI-42 INDEX™ can for example be accessed with Thomson Reuters Eikon. Eikon is a set of software products provided by Refinitiv for financial professionals to monitor and analyze financial information. It provides access to real time market data, news, fundamental data, analytics, trading and messaging tools. It also provides data on asset classes including Foreign Exchange, Money Markets, Fixed Income, Equities, Commodities, Funds, and Real Estate.

8. THE AI ANALYST PLATFORM

I think we all share the same problem: A great research paper is being published with highly interesting results, but the authors made it difficult for us to recreate or verify the findings, let alone getting access to the data or the source codes used in the papers. This is why I want to bring the AI Analyst platform to your attention. The creators of the platform have spent significant time and effort by incorporating multiple IP and intangible asset related research papers into one single combined platform, allowing users to use these results for further decision making. Access to the platform is not open freely to the public, but it is possible to request access by sending a request to office@42.cx.

8.1 DISCOVERING IP

The first use case of the platform is the IP research capability. At the time when this book is written, a combined collection of more than 200 million scholarly works, more than 110 million patent records and more than 100 million source code repositories could be searched, which represents almost all the patents, scholarly work and open source codes in the world. You would find segments of this data on a variety of other platforms like Google Patents or Microsoft Academic, but the main differentiator is that all data points have been associated and linked with companies (public and stock listed). This allows the user to, for example, find all AI-IP related patents belonging to a company, a sector or an entire industry.

Data is being collected from scholarly, patent, source code and financial data providers and includes sources like PubMed, Microsoft Academic, Crossref, USPTO, Orcid, OpenCitations, DOAJ, WorldCat, PMC, UnpayWall, GRID, WIPO, Core, GitHub, Nasdaq, CME, Quandl or Compustat. After logging into the platform, comprehensive searches can be performed:

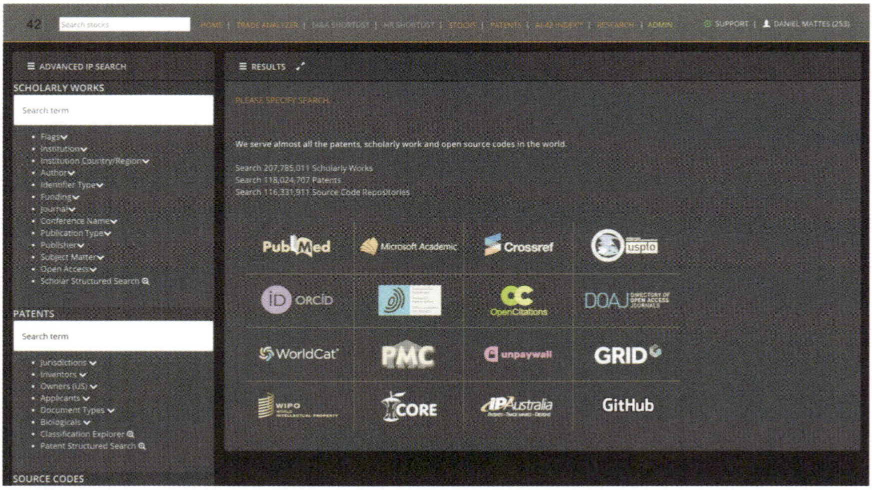

Advanced search functionality

It is also possible to review IP related to a specific company. For example, if we want to see AI-IP for the semiconductor company NVIDIA Corporation, we can search for the company by entering its stock symbol NVDA and click on the result:

AI-IP owned by NVIDIA Corporation

By clicking on a patent, the details are being shown, including the entire patent application, the images, claims and classifications:

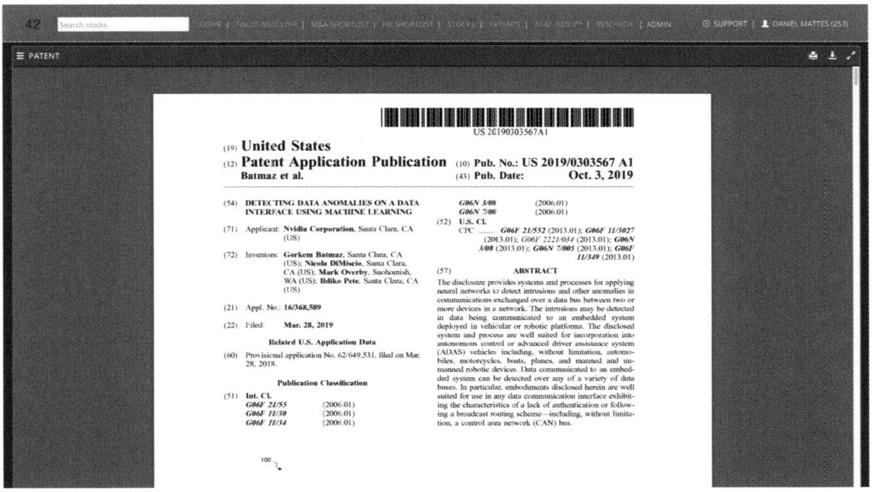

Details of an AI-IP patent owned by NVIDIA Corporation

With a few clicks, access to AI-IP based on individual stock titles and private companies can be discovered.

8.2 INDICATORS

The platform provides real-time access to indicators from IP and intangible asset related research papers, which have been implemented into the system. At the time the book is written, four sets of indicators are available, recreated from the following research papers. These have been identified as being especially significant for the purpose of identifying and measuring IP:

- **Mariagrazia Squicciarini, Helene Dernis, Chiara Criscuolo (OECD), „Measuring Patent Quality"**

The authors of the OECD paper "Measuring Patent Quality" propose patent quality measures with the aim to facilitate analysis both at the level of the individual patent and at the aggregate patent portfolio level. They are intended to help addressing a number of policy- relevant questions, for example, related to: firms innovation strategies and performance; enterprise dynamics, including the drivers of enterprise creation and of mergers and acquisitions; the determinants of productivity; the financing of innovative enterprises; the output of R&D activities and the returns to R&D investments; the depreciation of R&D; the output of universities and of public research organisations.

The chosen measure is their composite patent quality index, which is a combined index using the measurements number of forward citations (up to 5 years after publication); patent family size; number of claims; the patent generality index; number of backward citations; and the grant lag index. Only granted patents are covered by the index. Their Patent Quality Index(high) contains all stocks in the top 75% percentile.

It should be noticed that the original formulation of Lanjouw and Schankerman (2004) weighted the different components of the composite indicator using factor analysis. The OECD experimental patent quality indicators conversely assume all components to play an equally important role, i.e. they are assigned equal weights. This choice is motivated by the results of the exploratory analysis carried out when designing the indicator, which suggests that weights differ across technology fields and depend on the time span considered. Hence, for comparability purposes the composite quality indicators presented here assign equal importance to all components, and we leave it to future empirical analysis to determine the coefficients that would best mirror the relative importance of the different quality factors.

Needless to say, while the experimental OECD indicator tries to summarise a complex and multidimensional issue like patent quality, it nevertheless suffers from the typical drawbacks of all composite indicators, and should therefore be interpreted with care.

The OECD index is being updated and calculated on a monthly basis and is displayed in the platform with the following schema:

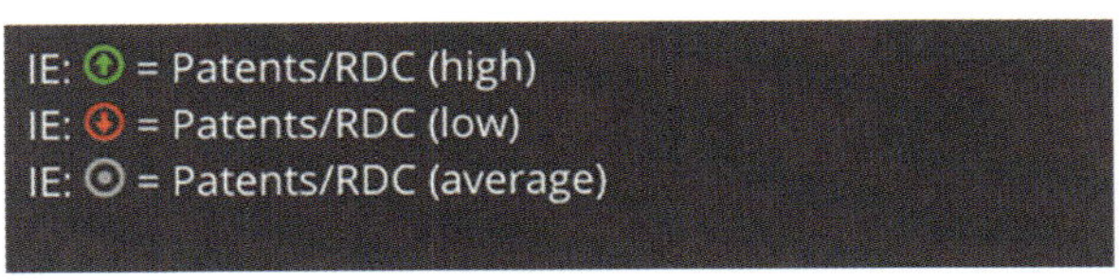

Platform indicators

- **Lauren Cohen, Karl Diether, Christopher Malloy (Harvard), "Misvaluing Innovation"**

The authors of the paper "Misvaluing Innovation" demonstrate that a firm's ability to innovate is predictable, persistent, and relatively simple to compute, and yet the stock market ignores the implications of past successes when valuing future innovation. We show that two firms that invest the exact same in research and development (R&D) can have quite divergent, but predictably divergent, future paths. Our approach is based on the simple premise that while future outcomes associated with R&D investment are uncertain, the past track records of firms may give insight into their potential for future success. We show that a long-short portfolio strategy that takes advantage of the information in past track records earns abnormal returns of roughly 11 percent per year. Importantly, these past track records also predict divergent future real outcomes in patents, patent citations, and new product innovations.

The main concept is to measure a company's "Ability" and "R&D to Revenue Ratio". "Ability" is meant to capture how good a firm is at turning R&D expenditures into something the firm values. We have run our tests using a number of measures of what the firm "values" and our results are robust to the various measures we have tried. We compute firm "Ability" by running rolling firm-by-firm regressions of firm-level sales growth (defined as log(Sales t/Sales t-1)) on lagged R&D (R&D t-j/Sales t-j; where j=1,2,3,4,5). We run separate regressions for 5 different lags of R&D (i.e., R&D from years t-1, t-2, t-3, t-4, and t-5); we then take the average of these five R&D regression coefficients as our measure of ability. The abilities for all companies are clustered Quintiles (0-4). Ability(high) contains all stocks in the top quintile (4).

The "R&D to Revenue Ratio" is being calculated by scaling R&D by sales. R&D(low) contains all stocks below the 30th percentile in R&D (but who have R&D greater than zero), and R&D(high) contains all stocks above the 70th percentile (>7) in R&D . We compute firm-year ability using the annual average of the rolling regression coefficients of sales growth on 5 lags of R&D (scaled by sales).A company is considered "Good", when a both metrics, Ability and R&D to Revenue are in the highest clusters and perform multiple stock portfolio tests. They find that the market consistently misvalues innovation in an ex-ante, predictable way. Specifically, the market does not take into account the information in firms' past R&D abilities. Firms that have been successful in the past and that invest heavily in R&D as a percentage of sales ("GoodR&D" firms) earn substantially higher future stock returns than firms that invest identical amounts in R&D, but that have poor past track records ("BadR&D" firms). A portfolio of GoodR&D firms earns equal- and value-weighted excess returns of 135 basis points per month (t=2.76) and 122 basis points per month (t=2.61), and 4-factor alphas of 90 basis points per month (t=3.11) and 78 basis points per month (t=2.27), respectively. In contrast, the portfolio of firms with poor past track records but that invests the same amount of R&D (BadR&D) earns -15 basis points per month in 4-factor value-weighted alpha (t=0.56). The spread portfolio that takes identical high R&D-level portfolios, but exploits differences in past track records, has a 4-factor alpha of 93 basis points per month (t=2.30) or over 11% per year. Returns to the "GoodR&D" (and spread) portfolios are large and significant in the first year, and then returns remain slightly positive but basically plateau in the second and third years, with no reversal. This suggests that we are not capturing a form of overreaction, but instead that the embedded information regarding innovation that the market is misvaluing is important for fundamental firm value. The following chart shows the excess return of their "high ability / high R&D" portfolio:

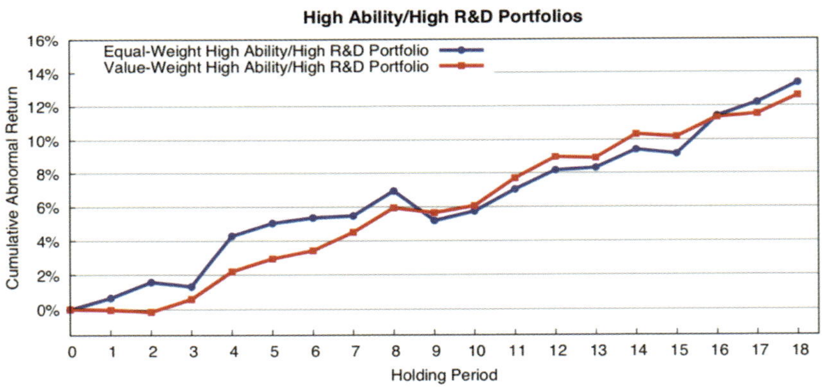

To summarize, in their paper they demonstrate that firm-level innovation is predictable, persistent, and relatively simple to compute, and yet the stock market ignores the implications of publicly available information when setting prices. Their approach is based on the simple idea that some firms are likely to be skilled at certain activities, and some are not, and this skill may be persistent over time. Hence, past track records associated with a given activity represent a straightforward way to gauge the future prospects of firms. Using this idea as the starting point for their analysis, they examine the predictability of firm-level R&D track records for future returns and future real outcomes. They show that despite the uncertainty typically associated with R&D investment, substantial return predictability exists by exploiting the information in these firm-level track records. They find that a long-short portfolio strategy that takes advantage of the information in past track records yields abnormal returns of 11 percent per annum. In doing so, they add to a growing literature showing that the market appears to underreact to the information contained in R&D investments. Their tests pinpoint a specific channel through which the market under-reacts to firm-level R&D investments by highlighting the importance of the interaction between a successful past track record and current R&D activity.

They show that the firms they classify as high ability based on their past track records also produce tangible results with their research and development efforts. In particular, R&D spending by high ability firms leads to increased numbers of patents, patent citations, and new product innovations by these firms in the future. The same level of R&D investment by low ability firms does not. Additionally, they document that high R&D ability firms that continue to spend substantial amounts on other activities, such as capital expenditures or total expenses as opposed to R&D, do not experience high future returns. These results suggest that their findings are unlikely to be driven by firms that simply anticipate higher sales growth in the future, and hence ramp up R&D and other firm-level activities in advance of sales growth. Rather, their findings are consistent with the idea that the firms they define as high ability are in fact truly skilled at R&D, and that future firm-level innovation by these firms is unanticipated by the market.

Given the substantial shift in the funding of research and development from the public sector to the private sector over the past few decades, the extent to which the stock market properly values investments in R&D is increasingly important. Their findings suggest that while R&D investment is indeed associated with considerable uncertainty, it is possible to identify potential winners and losers solely based on publicly available information. The fact that the stock market fails to adequately incorporate this type of information raises important questions about the efficiency of R&D investment in the economy.

The Harvard index is being updated and calculated on an annual basis and is displayed in the platform with the following schema:

Platform indicators

- **David Hirshleifer, Po-Hsuan Hsu, Dongmei Li (University of California, University of Hong Kong), „Innovative efficiency and stock returns"**

The authors of the paper "Innovative efficiency and stock returns" are focusing on the efficiency of turning R&D expenses into IP and patents. They find that innovative efficiency (IE), patents or citations scaled by research and development expenditures, is a strong positive predictor of future returns after controlling for firm characteristics and risk. The IE-return relation is associated with the loading on a mispricing factor, and the high Sharpe ratio of the Efficient Minus Inefficient (EMI) portfolio suggests that mispricing plays an important role. Further tests based upon attention and uncertainty proxies suggest that limited attention contributes to the effect. The high weight of the EMI portfolio return in the tangency portfolio suggests that IE captures incremental pricing effects relative to well-known factors.

The main concept is to measure a company's "Patents to R&D capital" and "Citations to R&D". Patents/RDC is defined as the ratio of firm i's patents granted in year t (Patentsi,t) scaled by its R&D capital [the 5-year cumulative R&D expenses assuming an annual depreciation rate of 20% as in Chan, Lakonishok, and Sougiannis (2001) and Lev, Sarath, and Sougiannis (2005)] in fiscal year ending in year t-2. We allow a 2-year gap between R&D capital and patents granted as it takes, on average, 2 years for the USPTO to grant a patent application (Hall, Jaffe, and Trajtenberg, 2001). The use of cumulative R&D expenses as the denomi- nator in this IE measure is premised on R&D expenses over the preceding 5 years all contributing to successful patent applications filed in year t-2 (which are approved in year t with the 2-year application-grant lag). Patents/RDC(high) contains all stocks in the top 66% percentile.

The second metric, "Citations/RD", is analysing the firms citations to R&D performance. To make sure the IE measure is fully observable to investors at the time of their investments, they follow the literature by using the citations received in the year before the forecast period by a firm's patents that were granted over the previous 5 years. Specifically, they define Citations/RD in year t as the adjusted number of citations occurring in year t to firm i's patents granted over the previous 5 years scaled by the sum of corresponding R&D expenses. The denominator, the sum of R&D expenses in years t-3 to t-7, is premised on only contemporaneous R&D expenses contributing to successful patent applications and a 2-year application-grant lag. For example, for patents granted in year t-1, they assume the associated innovative input is R&D expenses incurred in year t-3. They also set missing R&D to zero in computing the denominator. Citations/RD(high) contains all stocks in the top 66% percentile.

They also run portfolio simulations to validate the approach and find that average monthly size-adjusted portfolio return net of the one-month Treasury bill rate (excess returns) increases monotonically with IE for both IE measures. Specifically, for Patents/RDC, the monthly size-adjusted excess returns on the low, middle, and high IE portfolios are 49 basis points (t ¼ 1.48), 86 basis points (t ¼ 2.78), and 90 basis points (t 1⁄4 2.79), respectively. For Citations/RD, the monthly size-adjusted excess returns on the low, middle, and high IE portfolios are 59 basis points (t1⁄41.86), 81 basis points (t1⁄42.78), and 85 basis points (t 1⁄4 2.65), respectively. Furthermore, the return spread between the high and low IE portfolios is significant at the 1% level for both IE:

	Excess return (percent)	Carhart four-factor model plus UMO						Investment-based three-factor model plus UMO				
IE		α (percent)	*MKT*	*SMB*	*HML*	*MOM*	*UMO*	α (percent)	*MKT*	*INV*	*ROE*	*UMO*
Panel A: *Patents/RDC*												
Low	0.49	−0.13	1.06	0.57	−0.09	−0.02	−0.10	0.15	1.08	−0.07	−0.34	−0.08
t	(1.48)	(−1.43)	(42.16)	(15.73)	(−1.86)	(−0.74)	(−2.21)	(1.11)	(26.26)	(−0.75)	(−4.62)	(−0.92)
Middle	0.86	0.14	1.05	0.50	−0.25	−0.06	0.14	0.38	1.07	−0.02	−0.30	0.02
t	(2.78)	(1.42)	(41.36)	(10.91)	(−4.64)	(−1.89)	(2.43)	(2.77)	(27.82)	(−0.19)	(−3.00)	(0.21)
High	0.90	0.22	1.06	0.53	−0.25	−0.06	0.08	0.50	1.08	−0.04	−0.37	0.00
t	(2.79)	(2.52)	(41.12)	(10.88)	(−4.97)	(−2.18)	(1.51)	(3.68)	(27.63)	(−0.43)	(−3.86)	(0.03)
Panel B: *Citations/RD*												
Low	0.59	−0.05	1.04	0.55	−0.10	−0.01	−0.06	0.21	1.06	−0.02	−0.31	−0.07
t	(1.86)	(−0.55)	(38.61)	(13.16)	(−1.89)	(−0.41)	(−1.11)	(1.52)	(24.58)	(−0.22)	(−3.68)	(−0.72)
Middle	0.81	0.04	1.05	0.45	−0.16	−0.08	0.18	0.22	1.06	0.04	−0.22	0.05
t	(2.78)	(0.40)	(48.59)	(14.16)	(−3.65)	(−2.64)	(4.32)	(1.85)	(29.06)	(0.51)	(−3.11)	(0.60)
High	0.85	0.24	1.04	0.49	−0.28	−0.06	0.03	0.51	1.07	−0.09	−0.37	−0.03
t	(2.65)	(2.67)	(40.42)	(10.17)	(−5.25)	(−1.97)	(0.51)	(3.84)	(28.60)	(−0.89)	(−3.98)	(−0.34)

They find that firms that are more efficient in innovation on average have higher contemporaneous market valuations and superior future operating performance, market valuation, and stock returns. The relation between innovative efficiency (IE) and operating performance is robust to controlling for innovation-related variables suggested by other studies, such as R&D-to-market equity, significant R&D growth, patent-to-market equity, and change in adjusted patent citations scaled by average total assets.

Similarly, the relation between IE and current (and future) market valuation is also robust to a variety of controls. The positive association of IE with subsequent stock returns is robust to controlling for standard return pre- dictions and innovation-related variables.

Empirical factor pricing models, such as the Carhart four-factor model and the investment-based three-factor model, do not fully explain the IE-return relation. Adding the financing-based mispricing factor UMO to these models improves the models' explanatory power, but substantial and significant abnormal return performance remains. These findings show that the IE effect on returns is incremental to existing return predictors and cannot be explained by known factors (risk or mispricing).

Further analyses show that proxies for investor inattention and valuation uncertainty are associated with stronger ability of IE measures to predict returns. These findings provide further support for psychological bias or constraints contributing to the IE-return relation. The high Sharpe ratios of the two Efficient Minus Inefficient (EMI) factors also suggest this relation is not entirely explained by rational pricing. Finally, regardless of the source of the effect, the heavy weight of the EMI factors in the tangency portfolio suggests that innovative efficiency captures pricing effects above and beyond those captured by the other well-known factors and other innovation effects, which focus on either innovative input or output separately.

The fact that the mispricing factor partly helps explain the innovative efficiency effect suggests that there is commonality in mispricing across firms associated with innovative efficiency. Such commonality could arise, for example, if investors do not fully impound news about the correlated shifts in innovative efficiency that are driven by technological shifts. This is consistent with behavioral models in which there is commonality in mispricing (Daniel, Hirshleifer, and Subrahmanyam, 2001; Barberis and Shleifer, 2003).

As a policy matter, if capital markets fail to reward firms that are more efficient at innovation, there will be potential misallocation of resources in which firms that are highly effective at innovation are undercapitalized relative to firms that are less effective at innovating. Their findings suggest that investors should direct greater attention to innovative efficiency and that innovative efficiency can be a useful input for firm valuation.

The IE index is being updated and calculated on an annual basis and is displayed in the platform with the following schema:

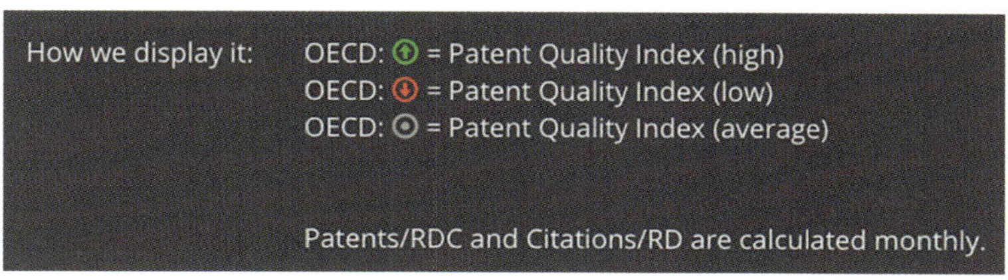

Platform indicators

- **Daniel Mattes, Jivka Ovtcharova, Gabriele Zedlmayer, „Using Artificial Intelligence to exploit IP related stock market inefficiencies“**

As discussed above, in our paper we demonstrate that analysing intangible assets of a company in great detail allows building a model to accurately forecast a company's ability to convert its intellectual property into stock value in the following quarter. We also demonstrate that a company's AI-IP impact correlates significantly with its future stock returns.

Our paper offers a new innovation-related measure, IPI, which is contemporaneously associated with market valuation and predicts future operating performance and stock returns. Existing studies relating to innovation and market performance focus on the effects of either the input (R&D) or the output (patents) of innovation separately. Our study differs in focusing on Artificial Intelligence based innovative efficiency as a ratio of innovative output to input, based on the idea that efficiency should be highly value relevant. We find that the predictive power of AI innovation is incremental to that of other innovation related variables such as R&D intensity, significant R&D growth, patent counts and citations.

We demonstrate that portfolio analysis confirms our hypothesis and show that a portfolio of top companies generated a return of 237% (+159% to baseline), which is significantly higher than the market (+78%).

The main concept is to measure a company's "Current IP Impact" and to generate a model to calculate the fair IP to market value. The Current Impact Index (CII) is calculated with the mean value of all forward citations of identified AI-IP publications of a company, published within the previous 365 days, scaled by the mean value of all forward citations of identified AI-IP publications of all companies from the same industry, published within the previous 365 days. This measure expresses the technological impact of a company's AI-IP compared to its industry peers. For example, a value of 1.10 would mean that the company's current AI-IP impact is 10% higher than its peers at the day of the calculation. Calculated monthly.

To create a robust AI-IP to market value model, we incorporate multiple parameters like R&D expenses, AI-IP, CII or revenue into the model. In this paper we are applying a Long Short-Term Memory (LSTM) recurrent neural network. We frame the supervised learning problem as predicting the stock prices at the current month (t) given the CII values at the prior 24 time steps (2 years), the R&D expenses at the prior 4 time steps and the revenues at the prior 4 time steps (4 months). As the OLS regression above showed, lag times for up to 2 years before can be an important measurement. The input values have been normalized and chosen because of the evidently strong correlation between R&D expenses, intellectual property and resulting revenues. For each of the companies, a dedicated Long Short-Term Memory (LSTM) recurrent neural network is being trained. Calculated monthly.

Portfolio simulations confirm the hypothesis. Panel A, all companies, generated an accumulated profit of +78%, which is representing the baseline. Panel C, the bad companies, could only generate +55% (-23% to baseline), significantly less than the baseline. Panel B, the top companies, generated a return of 237% (+159% to baseline), significantly more than the baseline:

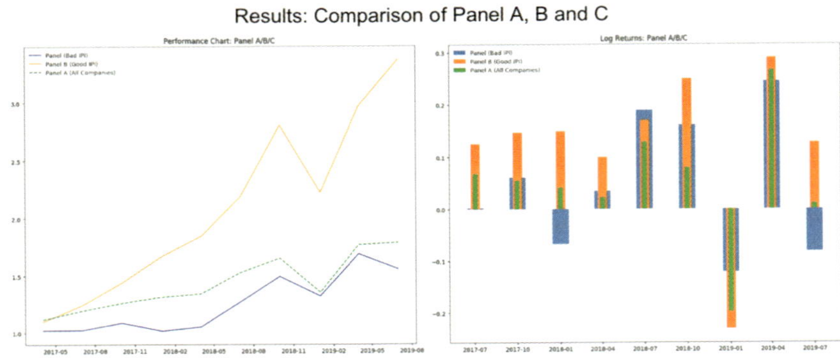

In this paper we demonstrate that analysing intangible assets of a company in great detail allows building a model to accurately forecast a company's ability to convert its intellectual property into stock value in the following quarter. We also demonstrate that a company's AI-IP impact correlates significantly with its future stock returns.

Our paper offers a new innovation-related measure, IPI, which is contemporaneously associated with market valuation and predicts future operating performance and stock returns. Existing studies relating to innovation and market performance focus on the effects of either the input (R&D) or the output (patents) of innovation separately. Our study differs in focusing on Artificial Intelligence based innovative efficiency as a ratio of innovative output to input, based on the idea that efficiency should be highly value relevant. We find that the predictive power of AI innovation is incremental to that of other innovation related variables such as R&D intensity, significant R&D growth, patent counts and citations.

It can be shown that lagged correlations of the introduced CII (Current Impact Index) for almost all of the industries are significant, as well as the correlation between the introduced IPI (AI-IP to Market Value Indicator) and the time lagged (t+1) stock price is significant in most of the industries. We find that a long only portfolio strategy that takes advantage of the indicators presented in this paper yields abnormal positive returns that portfolio analysis confirms our hypothesis and show that a portfolio of top companies generated a return of 237% (+159% to baseline), which is significantly higher than the market (+78%).

Our findings suggest that it is possible to identify potential winners and losers based on IP related information and that such information can add additional value to every asset management strategy.

The CII and IPI is being updated and calculated on a monthly basis and is displayed in the platform with the following schema:

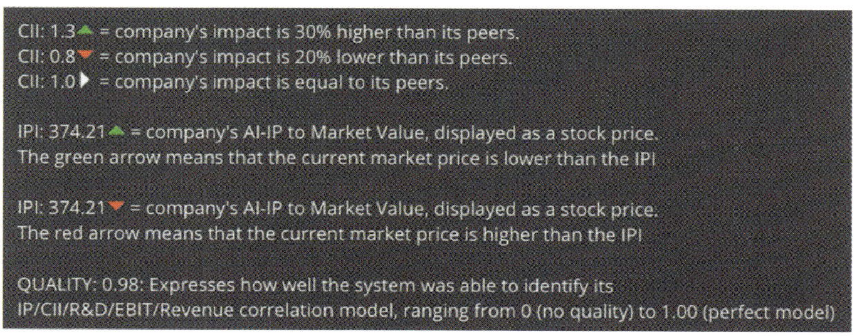

Platform indicators

8.3 STOCK DETAILS & INDICATORS

Company details can be retrieved by entering a stock symbol or the company's website. The firms' detail sheet consists of the following panels:

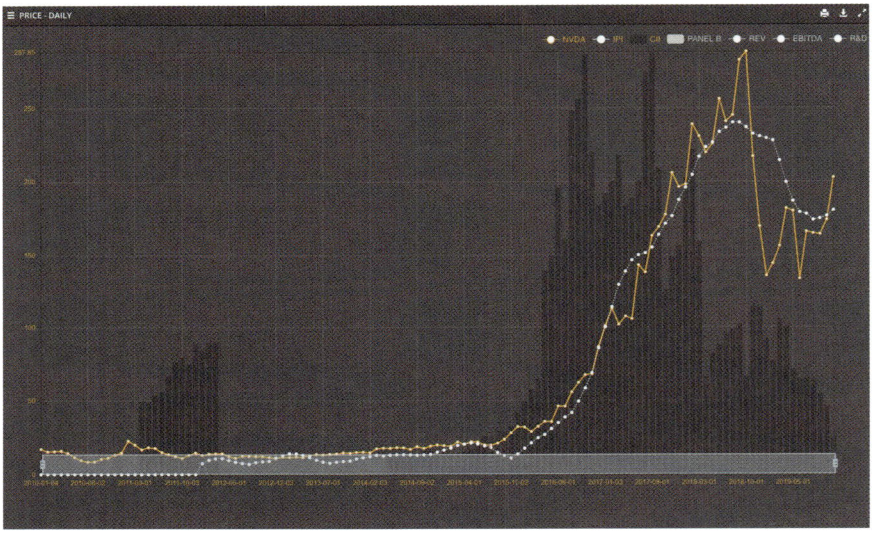

Chart panel

The orange line-chart displays the monthly stock price for the selected company over the chosen period. With the range scale element, the timeframe for the data displayed can be changed. The grey bars show the CII (Current Impact Index) for each month. The white line-chart displays the IPI (IP to Market Value Indicator) expressing the theoretical market value of the company.

Additional information like revenues, EBITDA or R&D expenses can be displayed in the chart, too by selecting them in the legend:

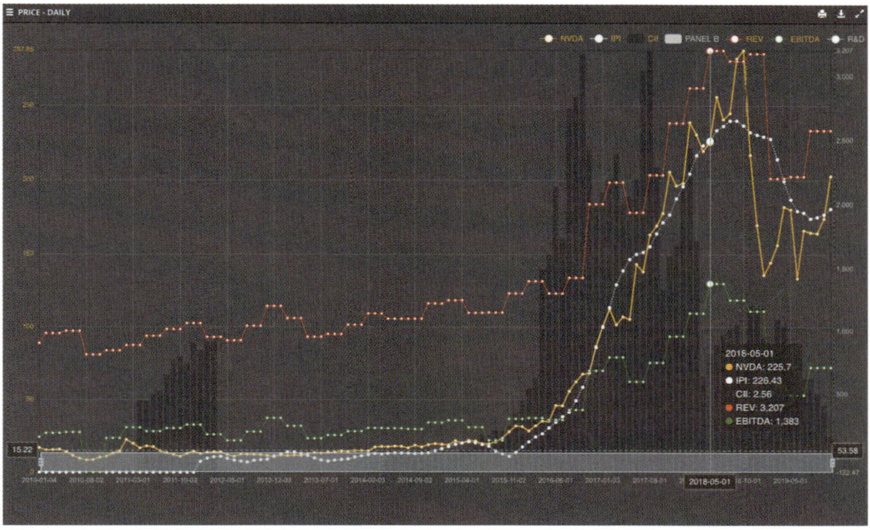

Chart panel with revenue, EBITDA and R&D expenses displayed

The panel "Indicators & Recommendations" shows the historical indictors for the company:

INDICATORS & RECOMMENDATIONS FOR NVIDIA CORPORATION (NVDA)

DATE	SYMBOL	ADJ.CLOSE	CHG	IPI	QUALITY	CII	HARVARD	IE	OECD	Revenue (M)	EBITDA (M)	EBITDA (% REV)	R&D (M)	RND (% REV)
2019-11-01	NVDA	202.59	0.16	180.59	0.97	0.78			[illegible]	[illegible]	[illegible]	[illegible]	[illegible]	[illegible]
2019-10-01	NVDA	174.00	0.05	176.67	0.97	1.44			[illegible]	[illegible]	[illegible]	[illegible]	[illegible]	[illegible]
2019-09-03	NVDA	164.17	[illegible]	174.99	0.97	1.71			[illegible]	[illegible]	[illegible]	[illegible]	[illegible]	[illegible]
2019-08-01	NVDA	164.75	[illegible]	173.99	0.97	2.01			[illegible]	[illegible]	[illegible]	[illegible]	[illegible]	[illegible]
2019-07-01	NVDA	166.00	0.24	178.00	0.97	2.04			[illegible]	[illegible]	[illegible]	[illegible]	[illegible]	[illegible]
2019-06-03	NVDA	133.64	-0.25	179.18	0.97	2.03			[illegible]	[illegible]	[illegible]	[illegible]	[illegible]	[illegible]
2019-05-01	NVDA	180.08	[illegible]	186.85	0.97	2.23			[illegible]	[illegible]	[illegible]	[illegible]	[illegible]	[illegible]
2019-04-01	NVDA	181.89	0.16	199.37	0.97	3.14			[illegible]	[illegible]	[illegible]	[illegible]	[illegible]	[illegible]
2019-03-01	NVDA	156.11	0.08	214.15	0.97	3.31			[illegible]	[illegible]	[illegible]	[illegible]	[illegible]	[illegible]
2019-02-01	NVDA	144.27	0.06	227.79	0.97	2.41			[illegible]	[illegible]	[illegible]	[illegible]	[illegible]	[illegible]
2019-01-02	NVDA	135.78	-0.19	229.29	0.97	2.88			[illegible]	[illegible]	[illegible]	[illegible]	[illegible]	[illegible]
2018-12-03	NVDA	169.50	-0.21	230.55	0.97	3.55			[illegible]	[illegible]	[illegible]	[illegible]	[illegible]	[illegible]
2018-11-01	NVDA	216.97	-0.24	232.27	0.97	3.59			[illegible]	[illegible]	[illegible]	[illegible]	[illegible]	[illegible]
2018-10-01	NVDA	287.85	0.01	236.77	0.97	2.09			[illegible]	[illegible]	[illegible]	[illegible]	[illegible]	[illegible]
2018-09-04	NVDA	282.22	0.15	239.99	0.97	3.19			[illegible]	[illegible]	[illegible]	[illegible]	[illegible]	[illegible]
2018-08-01	NVDA	245.05	0.01	239.99	0.97	3.09			[illegible]	[illegible]	[illegible]	[illegible]	[illegible]	[illegible]
2018-07-02	NVDA	240.85	-0.05	236.45	0.97	2.98			[illegible]	[illegible]	[illegible]	[illegible]	[illegible]	[illegible]
2018-06-01	NVDA	256.14	0.13	233.55	0.97	2.75			[illegible]	[illegible]	[illegible]	[illegible]	[illegible]	[illegible]
2018-05-01	NVDA	225.70	0.02	226.43	0.97	2.56			[illegible]	[illegible]	[illegible]	[illegible]	[illegible]	[illegible]
2018-04-02	NVDA	219.64	-0.04	223.25	0.97	2.08			[illegible]	[illegible]	[illegible]	[illegible]	[illegible]	[illegible]
2018-03-01	NVDA	230.73	-0.03	216.65	0.97	4.98			[illegible]	[illegible]	[illegible]	[illegible]	[illegible]	[illegible]
2018-02-01	NVDA	238.82	0.20	204.37	0.97	5.94			[illegible]	[illegible]	[illegible]	[illegible]	[illegible]	[illegible]
2018-01-02	NVDA	197.96	[illegible]	195.76	0.97	6.35			[illegible]	[illegible]	[illegible]	[illegible]	[illegible]	[illegible]
2017-12-01	NVDA	196.30	-0.04	187.49	0.97	4.89			[illegible]	[illegible]	[illegible]	[illegible]	[illegible]	[illegible]
2017-11-01	NVDA	205.61	0.15	176.61	0.97	4.67			[illegible]	[illegible]	[illegible]	[illegible]	[illegible]	[illegible]
2017-10-02	NVDA	177.63	0.05	171.43	0.97	3.94			[illegible]	[illegible]	[illegible]	[illegible]	[illegible]	[illegible]
2017-09-01	NVDA	169.15	0.03	163.82	0.97	6.54			[illegible]	[illegible]	[illegible]	[illegible]	[illegible]	[illegible]

PAGE 1

Indicators & Recommendation Panel

In this example, on September 3rd 2019, NVIDIA's stock price closed at 167.51. The IPI on that day was 198.55, which was higher than the stock price (indicated with a green "up" arrow), implicating that the stock is currently undervalued. The quality of the model is 0.96, which is very high on the scale from 0.00 – 1.00 and shows us that the LSTM was able to identify a robust prediction model between CII, R&D expenses and revenues to stock price, providing us with a confidence level of the accuracy of the calculated IPI. The CII on that date is with 4.75 above average (1.00), expressing that NVIDIA's AI-IP has currently more than 4 times the impact than its sector peers. Both Harvard indicators for January-June and July-December equally show that the company is in the Ability(high) and R&D(high) category. As for IE (Innovation Efficiency), NVIDIA is currently not in the average percentiles (neither high or low).

HARVARD INDICATOR (ANNUALLY) FOR NVIDIA CORPORATION (NVDA)

DATE	SYMBOL	HARVARD	Ability	R&D to Revenue	Ability Quintile (0-4)	R&D Percentile (0-9)
2019	NVDA		2.91	0.29	4	8
2018	NVDA		1.65	0.31	4	8
2017	NVDA		0.34	0.27	4	8
2016	NVDA		0.35	0.24	4	8

Harvard Indicator Panel

In the Harvard Indicator Panel, we can observe the results of the Harvard Good & Bad R&D metrics. In 2019, NVIDIA has been in the Ability(high) and R&D(high) categories for both periods, January to June and July to December. According to their research paper, the prediction index for January to June is based on the actual values from year-2, and the July to December on results from year-1. It can be seen that NVIDIA has been constantly in the highest Ability quintile 4, and in the higher R&D percentiles 8 and 9 (>7), classifying it as Ability(high) and R&D(high).

≡ INNOVATIVE EFFICIENCY (ANNUALLY) FOR NVIDIA CORPORATION (NVDA)

DATE	SYMBOL	IE	Patents Granted	R&D Capital (M)	Patents/RDC Percentile (0-2)
2019	NVDA		12	5233.56	1
2018	NVDA		8	4414.16	1
2017	NVDA		7	4033.39	0
2016	NVDA		1	3830.28	0

Innovative Efficiency Panel

The Innovative Efficiency Panel shows the results of the IE calculations, specifically the number of patents granted in that year as well as the calculated value of "R&D Capital" (RDC, as discussed above). The current Patents to RDC ratio is in percentile 1, which is average and doesn't classify NVIDIA in IE(low) or IE(high).

Further information, especially providing the development of R&D expenses or the value of intangible assets, is provided in the panels "Income Statements" and "Balance Sheets":

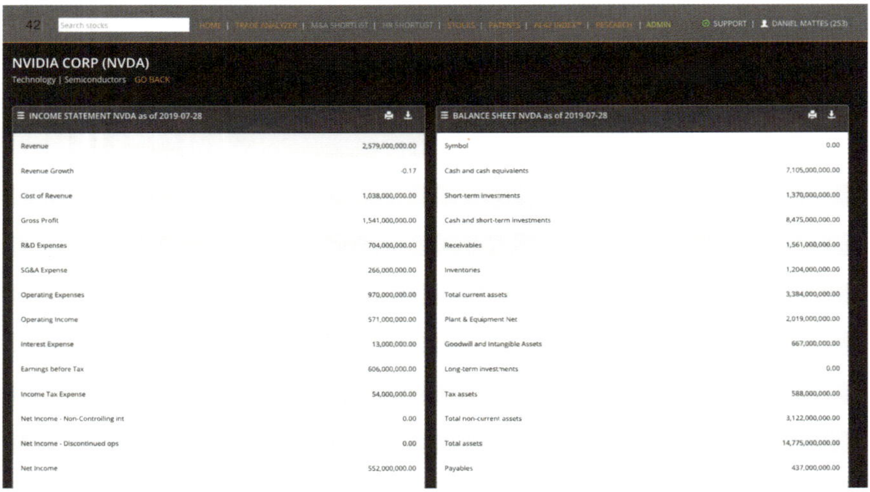

NVIDIA CORP (NVDA)
Technology | Semiconductors GO BACK

INCOME STATEMENT NVDA as of 2019-07-28

Revenue	2,579,000,000.00
Revenue Growth	-0.17
Cost of Revenue	1,038,000,000.00
Gross Profit	1,541,000,000.00
R&D Expenses	704,000,000.00
SG&A Expense	266,000,000.00
Operating Expenses	970,000,000.00
Operating Income	571,000,000.00
Interest Expense	13,000,000.00
Earnings before Tax	606,000,000.00
Income Tax Expense	54,000,000.00
Net Income - Non-Controlling int	0.00
Net Income - Discontinued ops	0.00
Net Income	552,000,000.00

BALANCE SHEET NVDA as of 2019-07-28

Symbol	0.00
Cash and cash equivalents	7,105,000,000.00
Short-term investments	1,370,000,000.00
Cash and short-term investments	8,475,000,000.00
Receivables	1,561,000,000.00
Inventories	1,204,000,000.00
Total current assets	3,384,000,000.00
Plant & Equipment Net	2,019,000,000.00
Goodwill and Intangible Assets	667,000,000.00
Long-term investments	0.00
Tax assets	588,000,000.00
Total non-current assets	3,122,000,000.00
Total assets	14,775,000,000.00
Payables	437,000,000.00

Panel Income Statements and Balance Sheets

NVIDIA's AI-IP and patents can be further examined as discussed above through the panel "Patents".

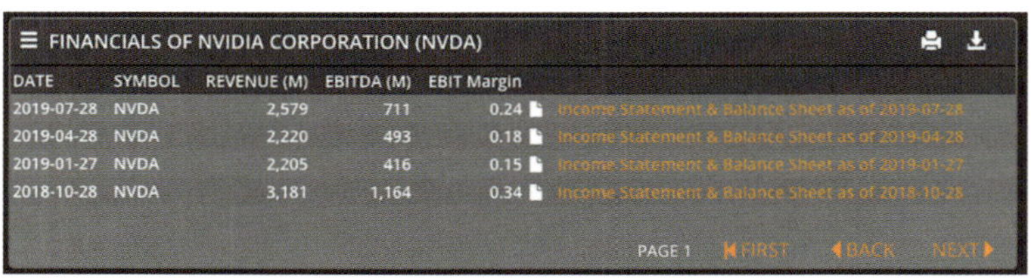

FINANCIALS OF NVIDIA CORPORATION (NVDA)

DATE	SYMBOL	REVENUE (M)	EBITDA (M)	EBIT Margin	
2019-07-28	NVDA	2,579	711	0.24	Income Statement & Balance Sheet as of 2019-07-28
2019-04-28	NVDA	2,220	493	0.18	Income Statement & Balance Sheet as of 2019-04-28
2019-01-27	NVDA	2,205	416	0.15	Income Statement & Balance Sheet as of 2019-01-27
2018-10-28	NVDA	3,181	1,164	0.34	Income Statement & Balance Sheet as of 2018-10-28

PAGE 1 FIRST BACK NEXT

Panel Patents

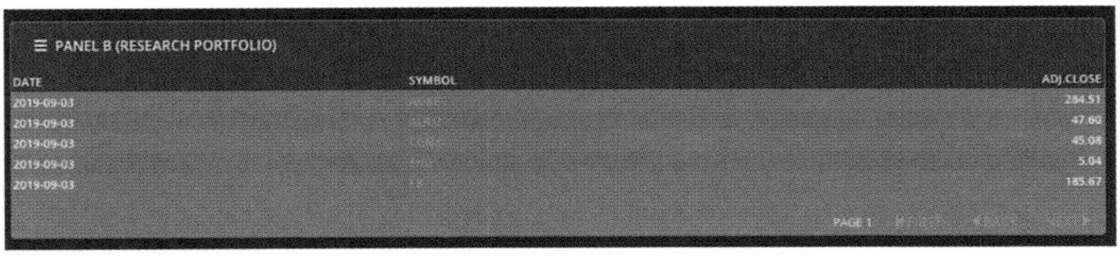

Patent Details

8.4 DISCOVERING OPPORTUNITIES

Asset managers and investors can use the information provided in the platform the access new type of information, which is usually hard to access and calculate. There is strong scientific evidence that analysing intangible assets and intellectual property of a company provides valuable information to form investment decisions. These can be used either stand alone or ideally in combination with existing strategies for the purpose of validating decisions.

Besides the possibility to explore individual indicators for sectors or stocks, the platform also displays a research portfolio ("Panel B"). This portfolio shows a portfolio, which is rebalanced each quarter, selecting stocks with the following criteria:

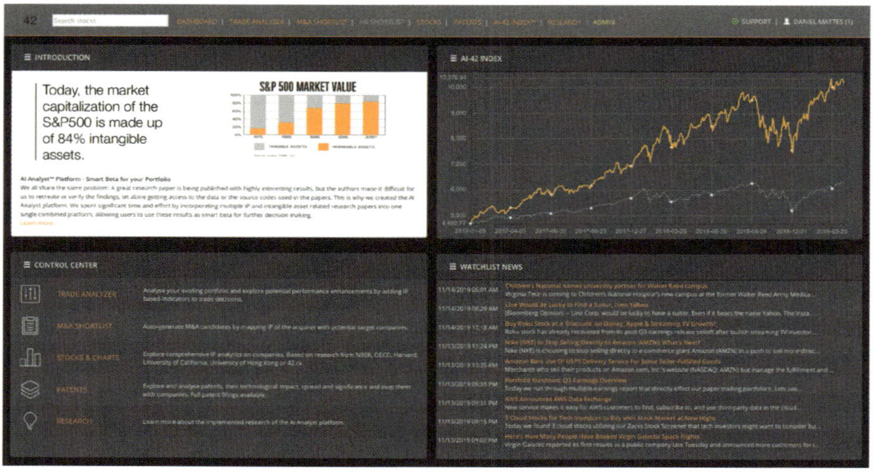

AI Analyst Control Center

At the beginning of each quarter, two measurements are being calculated: The positive gap between the current stock price (on an adjusted basis) and the calculated IPI of IPI models with a quality greater than 0.90, considering only IPI's of companies which value is highly depending on R&D, Innovation and IP impact ("IPI-GAP"). Stocks with a large IPI-GAP are potentially undervalued by the stock market.

The second metric is the forecasted IPI growth from the previous quarter to the current quarter. If the IPI grows significantly in a specific period, and the predictability quality is above 0.90, it gives a strong indication that the company's stock price will increase in the future ("IPI-PCT").

Stocks with an IPI-GAP greater than 1.00% or an IPI-PCT greater than 1.00% are being selected to be part of the portfolio. We perform this calculation at each beginning of a quarter, historically from 2012 up until today. The constituents of the Panel-B portfolio can be seen in the panel "Panel B Research Portfolio":

≡ PANEL B

DATE	SYMBOL	ADJ.CLOSE
2019-09-03	ALRM	47.25
2019-09-03	AMZN	1789.84
2019-09-03	IRTC	74.06
2019-09-03	NOW	263.38
2019-09-03	QTWO	88.15

PAGE 1 FIRST BACK NEXT

Panel B Research Portfolio panel

On an individual stock basis, Panel B participation can be also displayed in the chart panel for each stock:

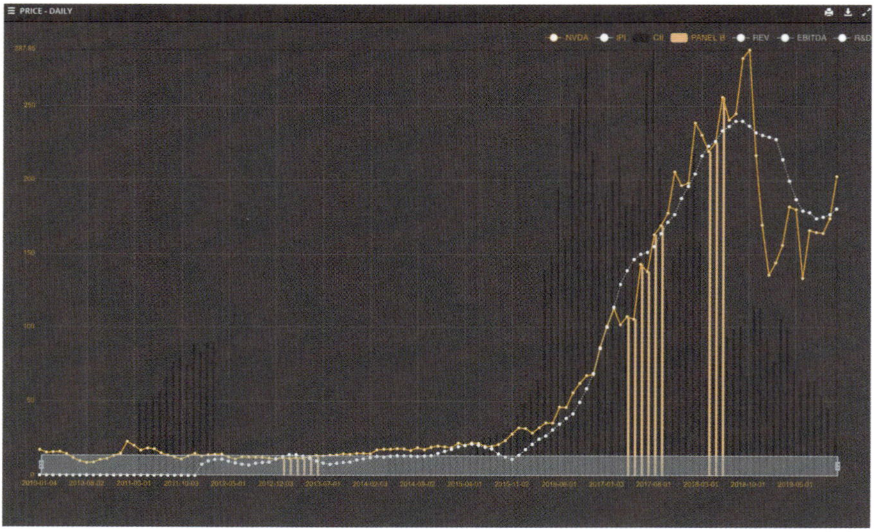

Chart panel with "Panel B" displayed

The orange bars highlight the periods where NVIDIA was part of the portfolio "Panel-B". This is a good example of how an investment opportunity based on intellectual property can be identified. In this case the strategy was able to identify accurately when to buy and sell NVIDIA's stock. In particular, the over-value situation in late 2018 combined with a predicted decline in CII was was followed by a massive stock price reduction and was correctly foreseen by the model.

Obviously and as with other indicators in the financial industry, none of the indicators are always correct, it is necessary to emphasize that also IP indicators should be applied with caution. But from out point of view, IP related indicators provide a novel and extremely interesting approach to be used in the asset management and investment decision process.

Indicators provided in the platform can be used to form variations of the research portfolio or can be integrated in existing investment strategies. Data can be easily exported as CSV files or directly accessed with an API for further use in 3rd party simulation tools.

Here are some additional examples of the Panel-B portfolio:

Adobe Inc (ADBE)

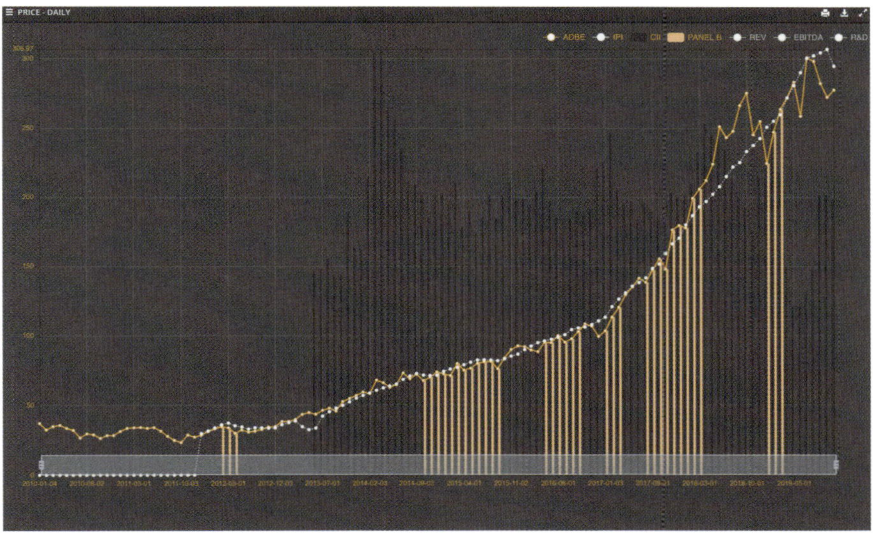

Chart panel with "Panel B" displayed

Amazon Inc (AMZN)

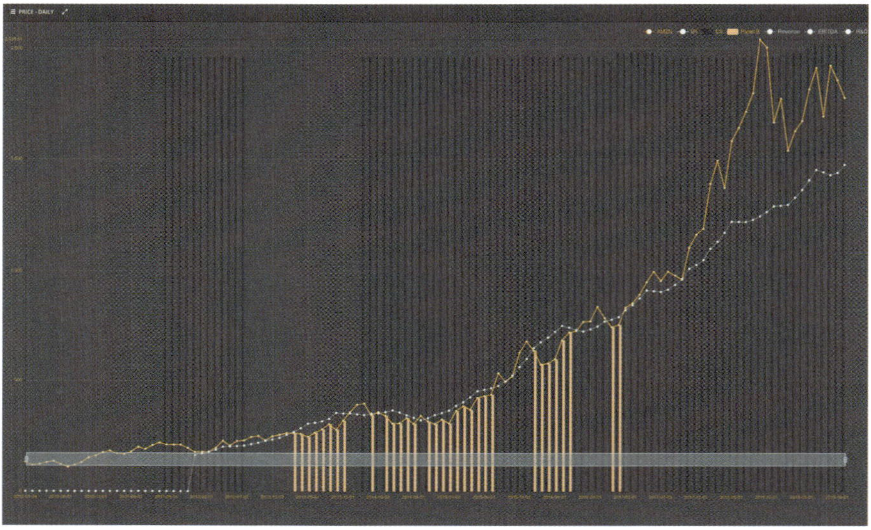

Chart panel with "Panel B" displayed

Microsoft (MSFT)

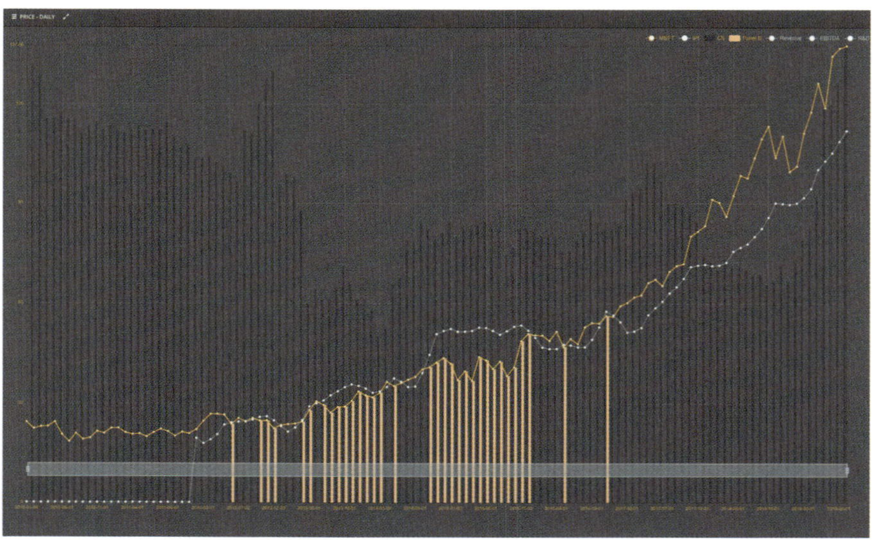

Chart panel with "Panel B" displayed

Salesforce.com (CRM)

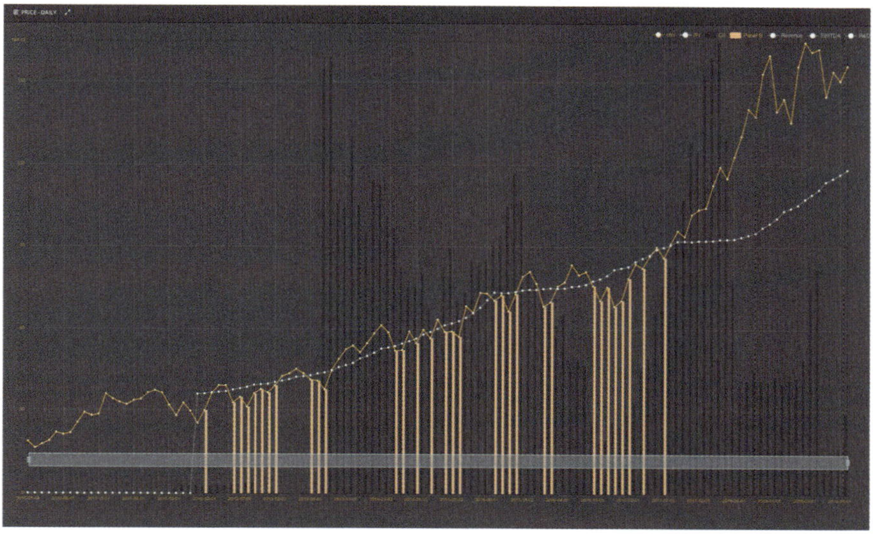

Chart panel with "Panel B" displayed

Paypal Inc. (PYPL)

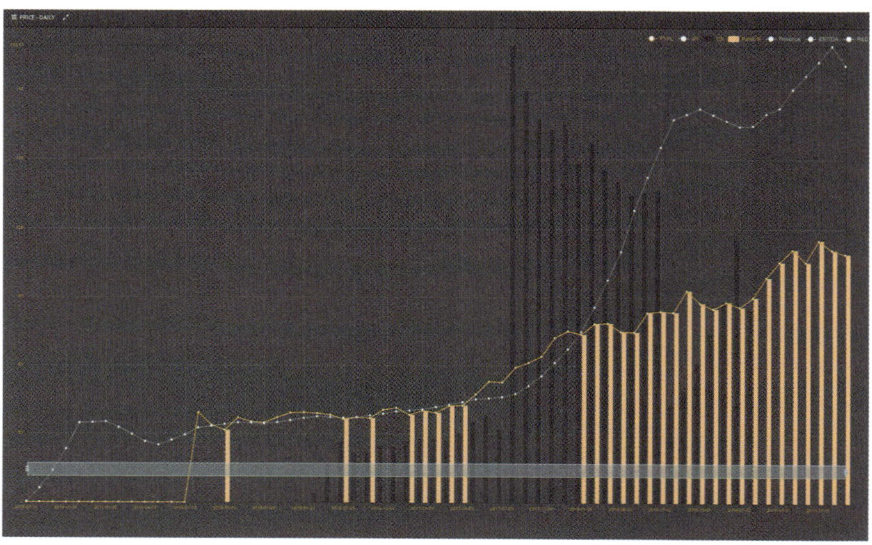

Chart panel with "Panel B" displayed

Broadcom Corp (AVGO)

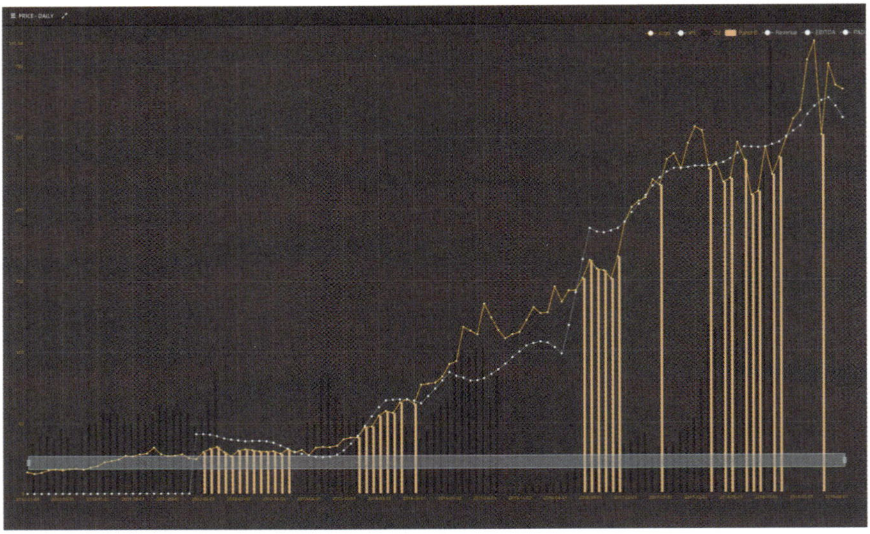

Chart panel with "Panel B" displayed

8.5 PORTFOLIO ANALYSIS

To discover how much impact the use of IP indicators has on an existing portfolio, trade analytics functionality is available in the AI Analyst, too. Asset Managers can enter all historical and current positions of a portfolio and will retrieve information about the IP indicators for each of the trades. If they are suggesting a "no trade" situation, a comparison chart is being calculated and the excess return to the original portfolio is shown. As each portfolio and its traded strategy is individual, this tool allows to specifically identify the potential alpha added by IP analytics.

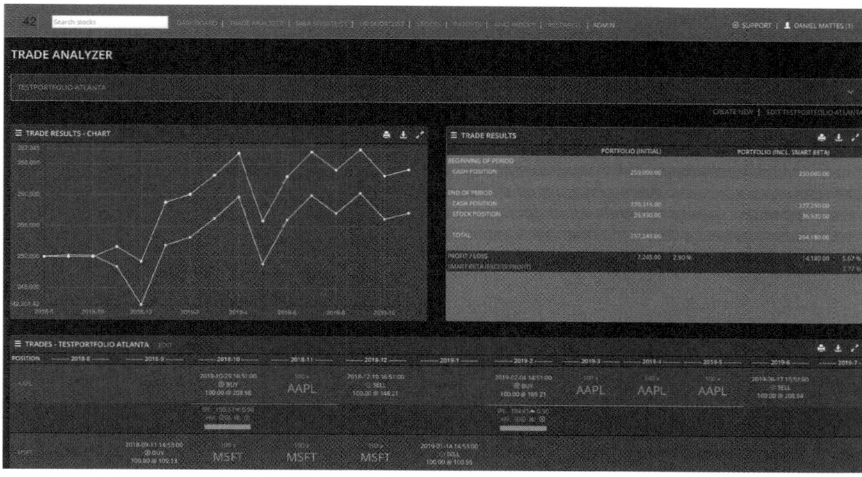

Trade Analyzer

In the example above, the asset manager's portfolio generated a total return of 4.39% over the entire period. Some of his traded positions could have been avoided if he would have used IP based indicators. The return of such an enhanced portfolio would have been 7.16%, which is significantly better than the originally traded portfolio. The chart visualises the historical profit & loss comparison between the original portfolio (orange line graph) and the enhanced portfolio (white line graph).

APPENDIX A: DATA

We combine a variety of data sources to create the sample we use in this book. We draw stock prices, volumes and adjusted prices from Quandl. Revenue, EBITDA, R&D expenses and other relevant financial data from Financial Modelling, information about stocks, industry, capitalization and more is from Nasdaq and patent data is aggregated from the The European Patent Office's DocDB bibliographic data from 1907 - present: 81+ Million documents from nearly 100 jurisdictions, USPTO Applications from 2001 – present with full text and images, USPTO Grants from 1976 – present with full text and images, USPTO Assignments (14+ Million), European Patent Office (EP) Grants from 1980 – present with full text and images, WIPO PCT Applications from 1978 – present with full text and images and the Australian Patent Full Text from IP Australia, scholarly data is collected from PubMed, Crossref, Microsoft Academic, CORE and PubMed Central and source code data from Github. All data sets have been merged by associating the corresponding stock symbol as retrieved from Nasdaq.

Industries, Stocks, Revenue, EBITDA and R&D Expenses

		Revenue (mean)	EBITDA (mean)	RND Expenses (mean)
Industry	Symbol			
Aerospace	BA	21,371,051,282	2,225,051,282	886,000,000
	UTX	14,654,384,615	2,570,179,487	570,025,641
Agricultural Chemicals	SNES	50,357	-2,739,071.43	659,143
Biotechnology: Biological Products (No Diagnostic Substances)	CUR	67,038	-3,683,829.42	2,081,583
	HALO	28,531,627	-8,758,216.10	25,081,956
Biotechnology: Commercial Physical & Biological Resarch	INCY	198,463,000	9,501,000	135,910,846
Biotechnology: Electromedical & Electrotherapeutic Apparatus	MASI	154,057,983	42,898,932	13,909,701
	MDT	5,618,589,744	1,682,188,034	457,974,359
	VAR	691,810,846	147,150,436	51,296,214
	VRAY	9,563,050	0.00	3,371,300
Biotechnology: In Vitro & In Vivo Diagnostic Substances	IDXX	397,548,564	96,799,846	23,603,795
	VRML	602,053	-3,447,789.47	695,816

Biotechnology: Laboratory Analytical Instruments	A	1,236,444,444	0.00	110,923,077
	COHR	260,514,479	51,612,427	22,953,957
	HBIO	26,601,795	1,755,513	1,463,308
	ILMN	485,244,145	164,896,462	95,235,359
	PKI	536,088,573	102,011,650	32,484,863
Building Products	VSLR	41,895,364	29,839,500	678,045
Business Services	AKAM	474,311,103	166,065,128	34,118,667
	CNDT	1,465,000,000	-15,500,000.00	5,312,500
	EBAY	2,621,511,077	950,322,667	292,921,641
	FICO	204,221,231	49,189,923	23,011,974
	MCHX	31,284,748	-582,654.36	5,776,031
	PYPL	3,010,428,571	0.00	265,190,476
Catalog/Specialty Distribution	AMZN	28,030,435,897	2,539,512,821	3,140,282,051
Computer Communications Equipment	CSCO	11,843,888,889	3,551,094,017	1,508,410,256
	JNPR	1,145,411,641	180,538,179	249,492,564

Computer Manufacturing	AAPL	46,769,333,333	15,529,384,615	1,901,128,205
	FIT	385,720,667	859,667	61,140,515
	HPE	7,754,017,857	1,315,410,714	416,339,286
	HPQ	20,542,957,265	1,863,897,436	518,051,282
	IBM	22,730,051,282	5,400,794,872	1,430,179,487

Computer Software: Prepackaged Software	ADBE	1,387,004,538	426,712,786	245,540,863
	ADSK	570,464,103	41,236,752	167,474,359
	ALRM	75,455,048	0.00	15,133,714
	ATVI	1,385,820,513	403,846,154	193,666,667
	CDNS	394,809,154	85,173,017	152,743,248
	COUP	48,871,872	-8,932,191.49	11,742,915
	CRM	1,590,698,547	188,689,504	228,036,650
	CTXS	661,506,051	167,461,179	110,829,103
	CVLT	137,605,179	10,627,410	15,808,949
	EA	1,087,692,308	192,615,385	301,076,923
	EIGI	217,375,357	44,046,000	13,607,393
	INS	3,295,231	932,897	754,590
	INTU	1,197,854,701	426,111,111	204,752,137
	LPSN	48,106,949	1,571,897	9,080,282
	MDB	56,025,171	-19,473,571.43	19,717,257
	MDSO	92,220,846	13,631,333	21,165,615
	MIME	77,163,000	5,404,889	12,477,889
	MSFT	22,446,666,667	8,710,102,564	2,973,538,462
	NATI	291,882,103	48,040,923	55,440,231
	NOW	293,547,765	-7,119,617.65	59,771,647
	NUAN	434,598,923	67,618,846	64,504,821
	OKTA	75,022,829	-25,519,097.56	19,652,561
	ORCL	9,325,119,658	4,085,743,590	1,320,401,709
	RST	58,066,077	-2,137,820.51	6,694,667
	SNPS	552,040,641	118,858,872	187,961,188
	SPLK	193,236,426	-41,413,128.71	52,331,416
	SQ	572,250,526	-13,858,421.05	87,103,789
	SYMC	1,279,829,060	418,162,393	219,470,085
	TWLO	111,195,500	-18,092,222.22	32,734,444
	VMW	1,488,471,607	448,297,769	318,099,658

Computer Software: Programming, Data Processing	FB	5,975,235,294	2,958,382,353	1,200,176,471
	GOOGL	18,709,641,026	6,330,461,538	2,800,769,231
	TWTR	520,063,667	35,705,148	157,309,667
Computer peripheral equipment	FEYE	142,908,464	0.00	52,549,571
	FTNT	239,060,308	32,449,103	34,956,744
	IMMR	12,256,256	-536,589.74	2,690,923
	LOGI	570,022,410	41,417,359	35,090,256
	XRX	3,789,948,718	432,589,744	140,846,154
Construction/Ag Equipment/Trucks	CAT	12,845,358,974	2,022,000,000	512,538,462
Consumer Electronics/Appliances	IRBT	159,591,974	18,391,769	19,478,761
	KN	215,196,192	25,784,577	21,750,000
Consumer Electronics/Video Chains	NFLX	1,842,091,949	1,037,739,282	152,863,385

EDP Services	CERN	921,374,222	267,623,487	112,853,197
	DMRC	7,178,513	-2,581,820.51	2,931,641
	PFPT	82,925,176	-6,827,558.82	21,398,559
	RNG	96,428,143	0.00	15,914,107
	TYPE	44,844,872	11,456,359	5,886,256
	VRNT	248,779,299	35,800,462	38,395,393
	VRSN	247,456,308	177,975,615	14,952,615
	ZNGA	229,355,429	-13,921,057.14	105,893,143
Electric Utilities: Central	ORA	142,504,872	57,912,128	1,225,897
Electronic Components	KLAC	803,087,436	273,947,974	127,032,821
	NTAP	1,456,060,684	261,488,889	203,148,718
	PSTG	214,760,797	-38,504,440.68	64,519,983
	STX	3,080,000,000	613,162,393	275,555,556
	WDC	3,697,427,350	670,401,709	404,786,325

Industrial Machinery/Components	AQUA	327,929,364	34,633,636	4,356,909
	BRKS	136,070,692	17,111,897	11,186,128
	CGNX	118,717,786	39,253,333	16,521,026
	CMI	4,657,752,137	681,897,436	176,136,752
	CUB	321,403,359	24,267,513	7,946,154
	DE	8,187,290,598	1,518,598,291	352,441,880
	GPRO	307,649,538	-5,602,269.23	49,910,538
	GRMN	738,000,256	192,021,564	102,627,846
	KODK	435,307,692	33,730,769	16,346,154
	PI	19,125,053	-2,940,368.42	4,748,289
	SENS	2,166,733	-15,932,066.67	7,040,200
	TMO	4,098,100,000	844,029,060	152,471,795
	TNAV	46,108,256	-228,769.23	16,697,282
	ZBRA	590,302,829	88,623,205	59,306,752

Industrial Specialties	ALGN	242,315,795	60,505,359	16,626,974
	ISRG	617,817,949	239,030,769	57,594,872
	ZBH	1,459,002,564	366,374,359	69,851,282
Integrated oil Companies	CVX	46,703,769,231	10,285,307,692	385,717,949
	XOM	87,439,179,487	14,862,076,923	441,051,282
Major Chemicals	CDXS	16,491,256	-2,924,000.00	9,187,385
	ROG	157,102,538	27,110,487	6,186,897
Major Pharmaceuticals	JAGX	686,483	-5,714,656.72	1,441,647
	JNJ	17,861,401,709	5,513,401,709	2,217,427,350
	KIN	929,250	-14,316,000.00	7,279,750
	REGN	827,569,744	276,831,333	336,207,513
Medical Electronics	HOLX	636,162,205	156,609,769	46,752,103
Medical Specialities	NTRA	54,085,095	0.00	9,850,286
	VCYT	14,498,893	0.00	3,023,214

Medical/Dental Instruments	BAX	2,936,615,385	788,410,256	193,461,538
	BSX	2,029,153,846	165,230,769	233,871,795
	DXCM	102,481,308	-9,809,256.41	26,055,692
	MMM	7,585,384,615	1,997,641,026	426,000,000
	NVTR	6,478,151	-9,260,188.68	3,560,415
	RMD	436,278,179	129,694,590	30,965,000
	SYK	2,546,061,538	491,400,000	154,535,897
Multi-Sector Companies	DLB	250,938,949	91,383,872	45,888,000
	TIVO	173,140,438	0.00	39,003,375

Office Equipment/ Supplies/Services	DBD	815,270,692	33,740,692	26,380,436
	NCR	1,504,794,872	141,615,385	53,538,462
	PBI	968,313,385	179,900,641	30,165,000
Oilfield Services/ Equipment	SLB	8,922,128,205	2,020,948,718	248,641,026
Other Consumer Services	SFLY	237,254,564	27,151,103	31,265,692
Paints/Coatings	PPG	3,541,564,103	604,358,974	111,128,205
Plastic Products	ENTG	252,384,983	56,787,684	20,307,581
Radio And Television Broadcasting And Communications Equipment	MSI	1,407,888,889	355,623,932	147,512,821
	QCOM	5,375,282,051	1,836,487,179	1,168,205,128
	VSAT	334,681,179	50,726,573	18,930,128

Semiconductors	ADI	934,924,265	347,933,453	174,288,590
	AMD	1,379,512,821	100,538,462	313,923,077
	AVGO	2,225,965,812	791,068,376	402,923,077
	CRUS	231,514,385	48,485,974	51,733,718
	GSIT	15,507,667	0.00	3,444,795
	INTC	14,127,239,316	6,064,264,957	2,740,316,239
	MU	3,842,948,718	1,690,367,521	351,222,222
	MXL	55,563,487	4,838,718	17,869,821
	NVDA	1,511,973,197	407,098,897	360,673,949
	SYNA	291,863,179	31,833,231	57,082,923
	TXN	3,414,307,692	1,363,282,051	381,179,487
	VIAV	299,417,949	20,708,547	46,877,778
	XLNX	601,870,530	198,908,966	134,379,043

Telecommunications Equipment	AVYA	733,833,333	129,500,000	54,833,333
	CIEN	574,475,581	39,298,615	104,212,547
	ITI	18,954,692	-153,333.33	1,301,923
	NTGR	288,964,915	26,621,966	17,312,829
	PLT	228,436,897	36,619,564	24,268,795
Television Services	ROKU	183,609,125	-6,201,750.00	42,749,375

The table above shows: (i) The stock symbol for each industry; (ii) the mean value of the Company's revenues in the period between January 2010 and August 2019; (ii) the mean value of the Company's EBITDA in the period between January 2010 and August 2019; (iii) the mean value of the Company's R&D expenses in the period between January 2010 and August 2019;

Summary Patent Data

	#	Publi-cation Year	Cited by Patent Count	Simple Family Size	Exten-ded Family Size	Sequen-ce Count	NPL Citation Count	NPL Resol-ved Citation Count
count	268,571	268,571	268,571	268,571	268,571	268,571	268,571	268,571
mean	19,006	2,013.25	12.16	7.20	20.56	147.36	7.24	2.42
std	12,343	5.89	45.95	15.16	85.65	22,022	34.50	13.88
min	1.00	1,973.00	0.00	1.00	1.00	0.00	0.00	0.00
25%	8,393.00	2,011.00	0.00	2.00	2.00	0.00	0.00	0.00
50%	17,864	2,015.00	1.00	4.00	5.00	0.00	0.00	0.00
75%	27,963	2,018.00	7.00	8.00	10.00	0.00	2.00	0.00
max	48,947	2,019.00	4,761.00	383.00	4,857.00	5,305,026	2,192.00	780.00

The table above shows the count, mean, standard deviation, minimum, 25% percentile, 50% percentile, 50% percentile, 75% percentile and the maximum value for publication year, cited by patent count (forward citations), patent family size (simple and extended), sequence counts, NPL (Non Patent Literature) citation counts and resolved NPL citation counts.

Summary Patent Data

Symbol	Cited by Patent Count	NPL Citation Count	NPL Resolved Citation Count
000651	3	0	0
000725	1	5	0
005930	12374	3517	765
066570	751	104	36
2317	550	113	46
4901	1910	395	164
4902	77	141	63
6501	9678	1035	355
6502	5498	1001	416
6645	961	356	124
6701	4767	2216	966
6702	3363	1459	597
6724	373	167	121
6752	515	312	99
6841	113	41	12
6902	409	83	20
6952	398	131	31
6954	258	158	64
7733	84	84	43
7752	3806	4484	1573
7951	2651	501	253
8035	2065	659	120

8299	119	36	6
9432	454	172	58
9437	162	330	118
A	752	205	84
AAPL	14549	90313	23202
ABBN	1735	427	162
ACN	22522	5661	974
ADBE	1579	3500	1474
ADI	173	522	232
ADPT	94	7842	6383
ADSK	513	118	26
AKAM	275	9	0
ALGN	278	359	172
ALL	1614	3198	129
ALRM	14	3	0
AMD	4702	1309	367
AMZN	8078	10377	1674
APLS	392	2482	860
AQUA	5	9	1
ASML	145	194	61
ATVI	159	287	36
AVGO	883	290	108
AVYA	6190	2000	283
AXP	4236	971	267

AYI	332	1796	187
AZN	208	2731	2110
BA	4040	1716	660
BABA	369	290	73
BAC	679	329	45
BAP	36	171	83
BAX	886	725	68
BB	1013	271	50
BBC	632	754	190
BCOW	679	539	353
BHGE	1575	88	40
BIDU	918	536	72
BIOS	129	82	20
BMCH	79	26	4
BPRN	3	68	14
BRKS	467	92	23
BSX	3121	1229	186
BTI	5022	1155	449
BWA	30	80	13
CAH	113	2	0
CAJ	3440	1194	634
CAT	3993	889	451
CATC	2	138	109
CBD	0	0	0
CDNS	802	593	228

CDXS	170	1473	1001
CEL	384	36	18
CERN	156	639	105
CGEN	597	201	176
CGNX	559	850	436
CIEN	141	52	29
CL	1	4	0
CLGX	429	115	23
CMCSA	699	326	89
CMI	87	36	21
CNDT	63	534	254
CNHI	35	21	7
COF	116	330	85
COHR	251	676	35
COLD	54	145	138
COUP	2	7	0
CPAC	543	544	406
CRM	489	809	146
CRUS	21	18	4
CRWD	2	0	0
CSCO	10585	10942	2294
CSV	163	1332	214
CTL	88	138	16
CTXS	976	1616	433
CUB	31	15	2

CUR	248	128	61
CVLT	166	1171	237
CVR	268	140	8
CVX	186	60	35
CYBR	0	10	0
DARE	634	112	0
DBD	2017	28	1
DBX	263	116	7
DE	996	227	48
DELL	327	1273	87
DIS	358	619	386
DLB	456	1717	392
DLPH	1241	256	77
DMRC	2282	1629	622
DNJR	647	136	59
DRNA	62	173	122
DSY	154	588	368
DTE	724	402	213
DXCM	13251	6533	5526
EA	2288	451	103
EBAY	1279	5395	645
EFX	33	53	4
EIGI	837	46	4
EKTA-B	18	105	47
ENTG	88	168	4

ERIC	4167	915	289
ESLT	5	4	3
F	5842	4334	1320
FB	4054	11874	896
FCN	21	964	457
FENG	4991	1962	596
FEYE	1081	3211	904
FICO	693	331	111
FIT	3919	7387	1432
FLEX	7834	5187	35
FTNT	582	1331	128
FTSV	179	839	690
GE	15669	8847	5579
GH	7	11	10
GM	6418	397	212
GNTX	856	39	5
GNW	208	816	308
GOOGL	22144	36712	9181
GPRO	58	837	438
GRMN	1010	860	141
GRPN	66	302	26
GRTS	7	27	21
GSIT	2	1	0
GSK	3	843	509
GT	108	19	8

HAL	1811	790	242
HALO	53	6	0
HBIO	518	1314	963
HDVY	3717	6087	2425
HJV	45	0	0
HMC	4101	2559	925
HMI	6	37	15
HO	90	139	78
HOLX	9	114	61
HON	6140	1859	702
HPE	10780	2717	862
HPQ	28	30	10
HUBB	20	25	0
IBM	96990	47311	13489
ICLK	33	98	32
IDCC	111	38	6
DXX	60	33	18
EP	7	17	11
GR	20	6	0
LMN	954	1790	1229
MMR	589	608	188
NCY	536	587	522
NFY	421	103	31
INS	10479	301	43
INTC	5905	3995	1067

INTU	301	728	88
IR	126	23	4
IRBT	571	4894	1503
ISRG	960	448	139
ISTR	878	595	168
ITI	319	144	79
ITW	183	25	2
JAGX	17	3	1
JCTCF	497	670	60
JLL	17	400	190
JNJ	1173	132	32
JNPR	746	538	118
JPM	391	900	166
KIN	18	27	9
KLAC	487	316	89
KMB	3357	172	41
KN	55	1174	219
KODK	7895	685	333
KW	58	10	0
LHX	3364	429	127
LMT	3232	534	201
LOGI	236	143	11
LPSN	96	202	6
LPTX	124	1650	308
LYFT	8	34	2

MA	286	89	7
MASI	1023	253	57
MCHX	37	1	0
MDB	66	37	8
MDSO	25	69	18
MDT	8713	2435	1425
MESO	963	1632	54
MG	49	8	0
MGA	386	6241	3153
MGIC	1480	7756	122
MGTX	31	93	44
MIME	43	14	1
MMC	67	18	10
MMM	1146	591	265
MNRL	0	3	3
MNST	222	37	0
MSFT	149476	86961	26268
MSI	6978	1508	346
MSTR	1899	635	67
MU	3723	1207	245
MUFG	5525	1211	660
MXL	42	105	26
NATI	2468	1142	363
NCR	5989	308	142
NERV	317	203	171

NFLX	47	110	54
NKE	545	138	5
NLSN	1252	8175	1291
NOC	1016	206	88
NOK	3282	1095	300
NOW	8	37	12
NRE	0	0	0
NTAP	17	41	6
NTGR	6	0	0
NTRA	63	962	689
NUAN	902	2003	479
NVDA	479	353	160
NVS	183	183	119
NVTR	45	42	8
NXPI	38	55	27
OKTA	15	8	0
ORA	910	251	160
ORAN	4	52	28
ORCL	17670	5412	1410
PBI	1018	97	20
PDD	58	7	6
PFPT	107	78	2
PG	839	174	102
PHG	16421	2570	1244
PI	32	22	0

PKE	29	169	91
PKI	35	15	3
PLT	105	1	0
PPG	18	77	31
PSO	87	44	14
PSTG	46	230	27
PSV	222	49	12
PTR	1	6	0
PXLW	161	3	0
PYPL	80	970	100
QCOM	17442	5738	2588
RDWR	465	118	30
REGN	4	206	168
RES	107	38	0
RMD	3023	1295	36
RNG	14	9	1
RNST	2817	453	201
ROG	350	597	323
ROK	15744	5176	493
ROKU	3	9	0
RST	269	640	599
RTN	1503	1516	429
RY	119	295	15
S	1360	500	117
SAP	3853	2413	555

SCWX	956	273	44
SENS	100	297	48
SFIX	10	2	0
SFLY	37	0	1
SHI	107	365	284
SHOS	23	13	0
SIE	15685	4418	2366
SITE	81	14	4
SLB	4259	718	325
SNDR	2378	1776	202
SNE	8921	3132	855
SNES	107	1325	937
SNPS	304	198	127
SPLK	847	3174	189
SPOT	15	147	27
SQ	475	541	5
SRCI	805	1445	519
STM	2099	868	559
STX	476	145	94
SUN	4	313	9
SWZ	6	32	6
SYK	63	4	0
SYMC	4254	3774	726
SYNA	366	80	47
T	50218	97458	28080

TER	905	119	34
TIVO	944	1861	334
TM	1144	2137	981
TME	198	152	24
TMO	11357	5118	705
TMQ	572	7	3
TMUS	23	46	4
TNAV	134	52	4
TRI	1561	1639	739
TRMB	971	108	43
TSLA	0	2	0
TTM	312	356	123
TWLO	237	91	35
TWTR	107	159	34
TXN	8549	932	391
TYPE	48	119	3
UBER	165	610	134
UIS	1023	181	85
UPS	3447	1775	406
UTI	0	12	0
UTX	881	101	26
V	1036	223	26
VAR	26	40	28
VC	386	43	19
VCF	6260	65	0

VCYT	68	1130	784
VIAV	2	12	0
VMW	175	376	95
VOD	25	12	2
VRAY	2	22	13
VRML	11	330	300
VRNT	1050	6110	862
VRSN	75	211	84
VSAT	68	10	2
VSLR	31	8	2
VVPR	98	236	65
VZ	527	483	64
WAB	5110	191	58
WD	463	295	2
WDC	3	48	5
WHR	283	1	0
WIT	57	101	38
WIX	8	14	3
WMT	309	3081	257
WORK	0	0	0
WRTC	20	0	0
WSG	19	4	1
WTER	14	9	0
XLNX	1512	380	48
XNCR	666	787	709

XOM	460	328	185
XRX	34108	6161	2627
YNDX	53	156	35
ZBH	5	22	6
ZBRA	2868	57	21
ZNGA	30	154	2
ZS	141	18	16

The table above shows for each company: (i) the aggregated number of forward citations (Cited by Patent Count); (ii) the aggregated number of Non Patent Literature (NPL) citations; (iii) the aggregated number of resolved Non Patent Literature (NPL) citations;

APPENDIX B: AI-IP TO MARKET VALUE INDICATOR (IPI) CHARTS

AAPL

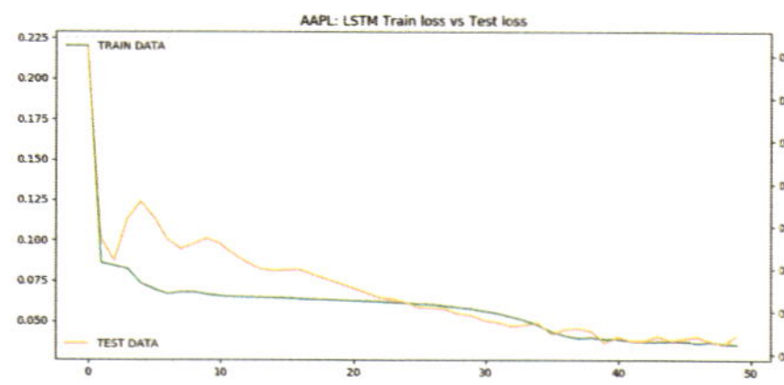

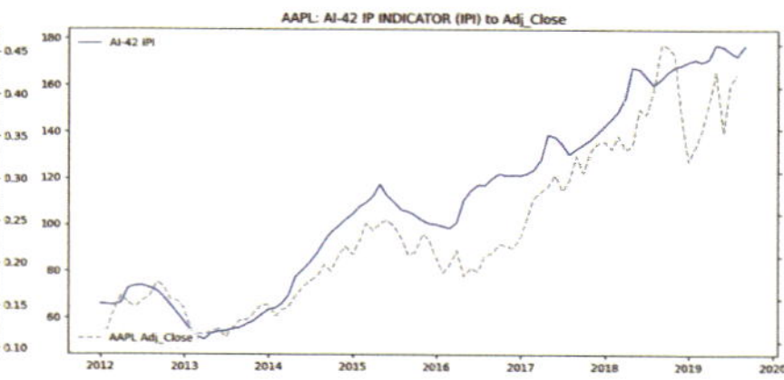

ADBE

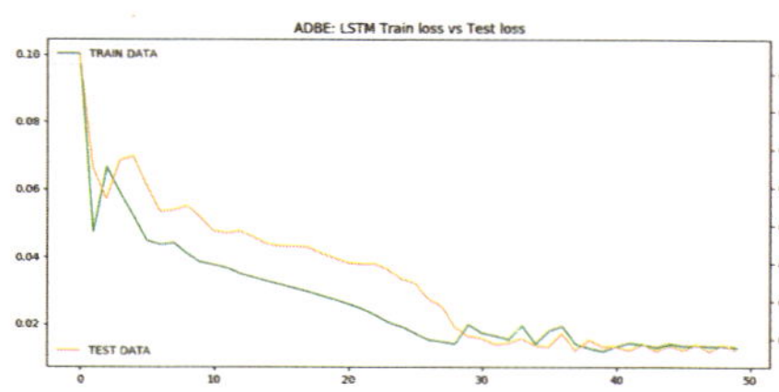

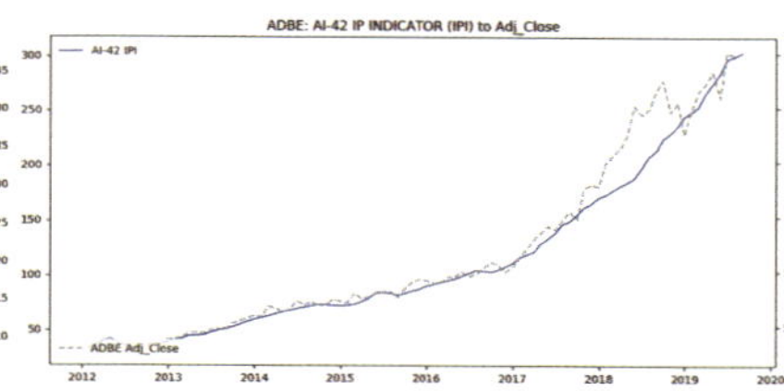

ADI

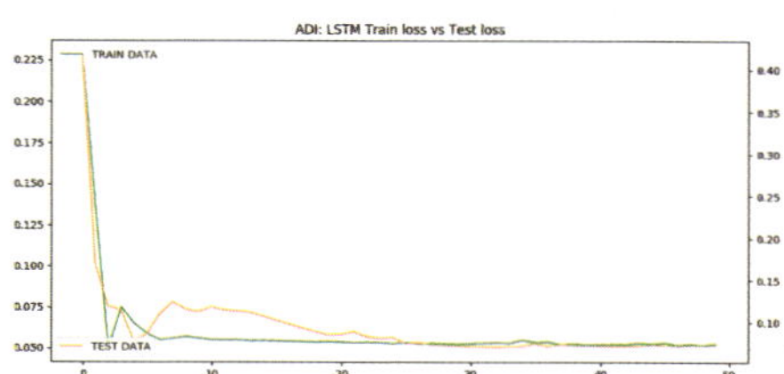

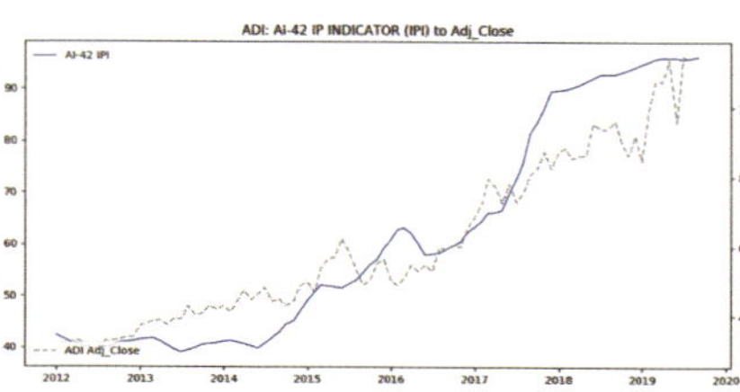

ISTR

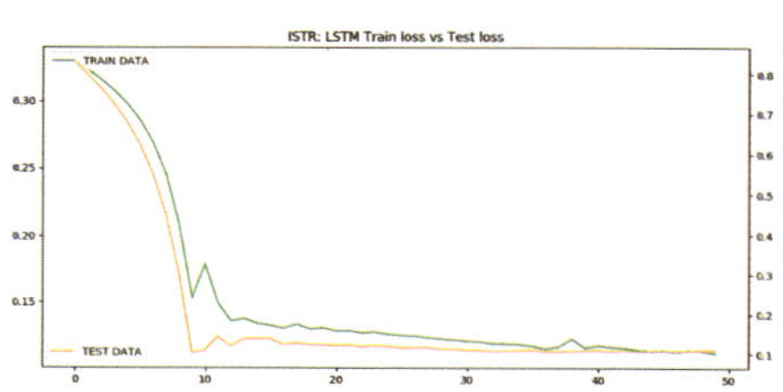

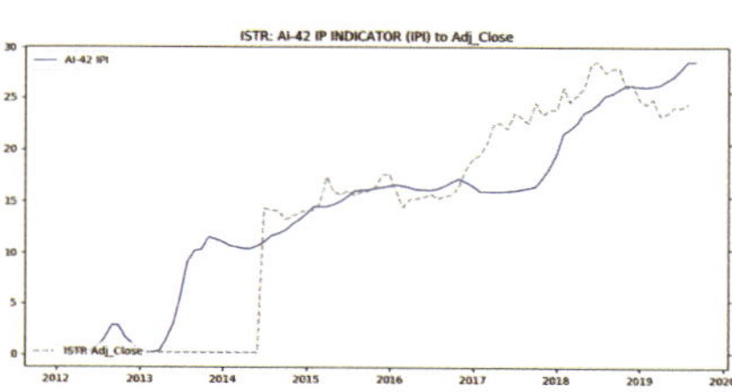

GRMN

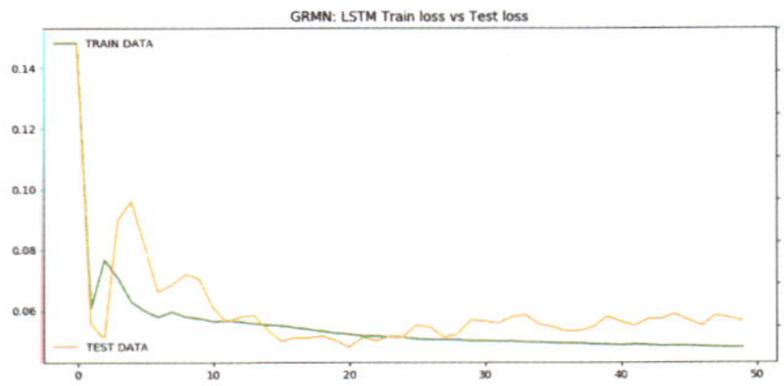

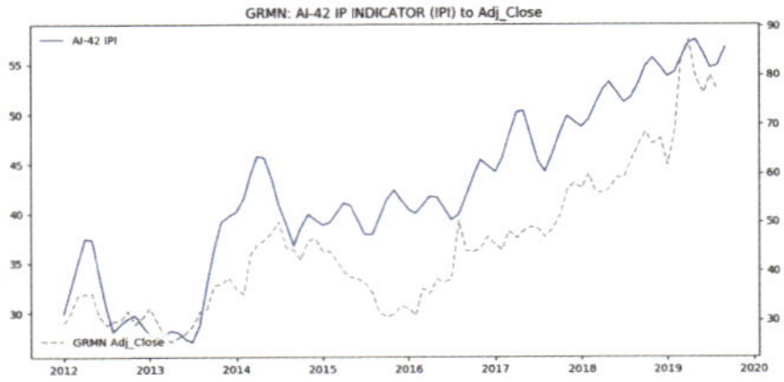

XNCR

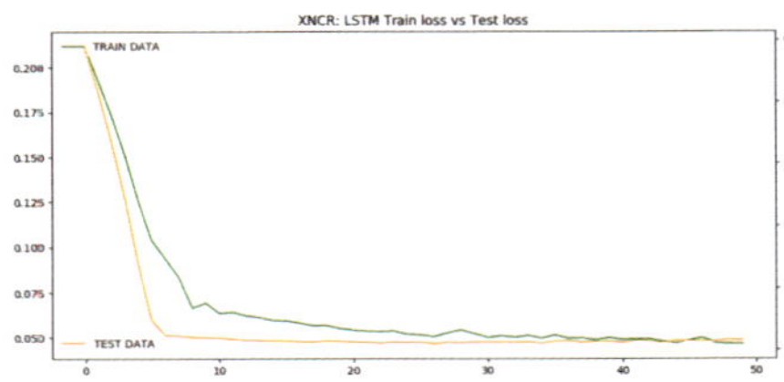

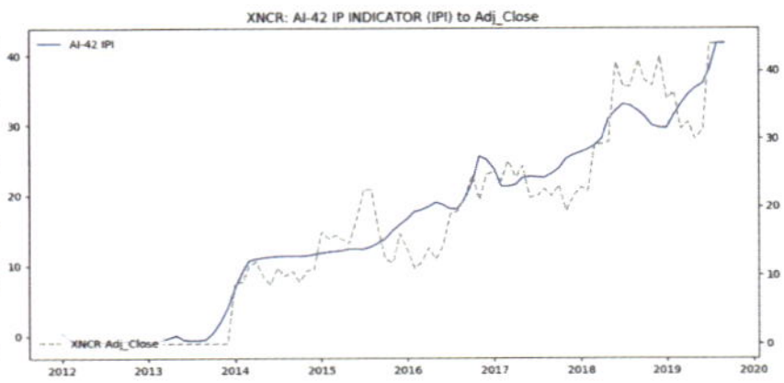

SCWX

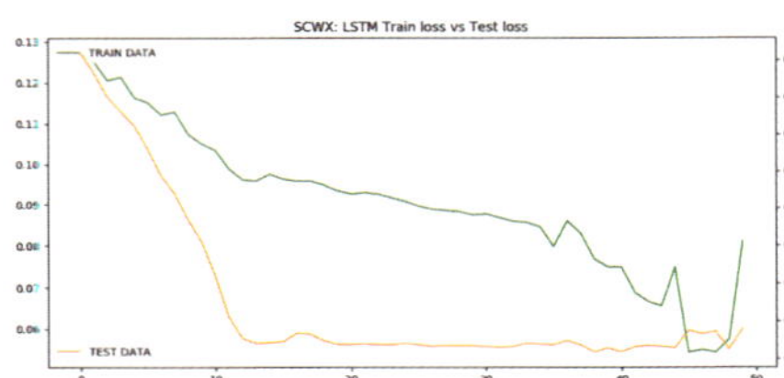

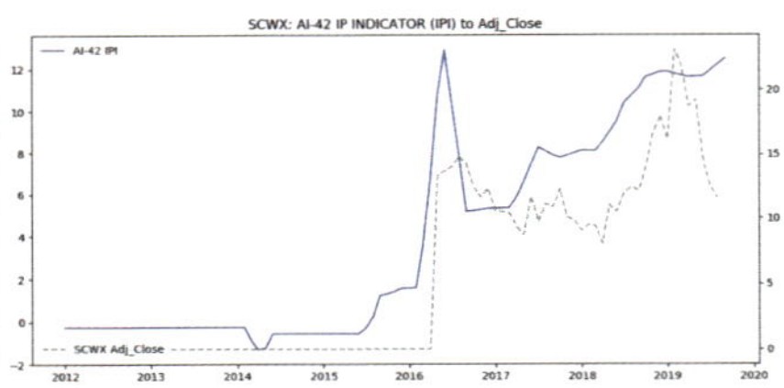

ORA

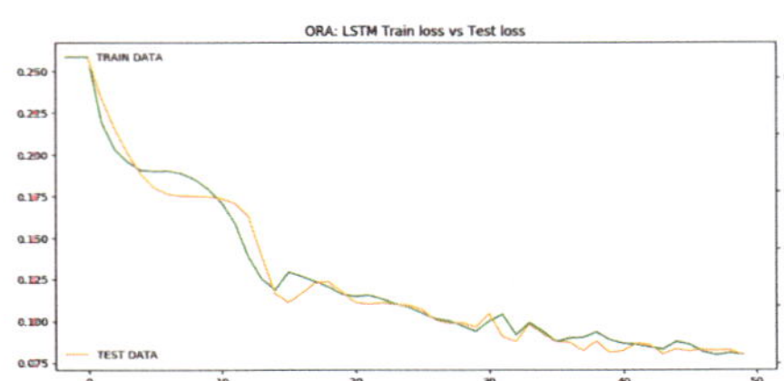

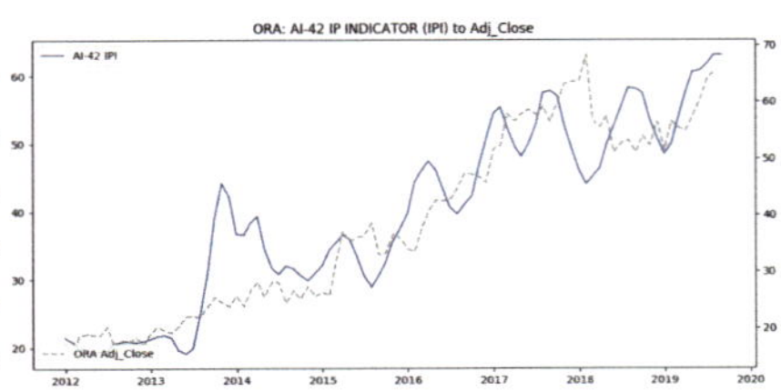

CVR

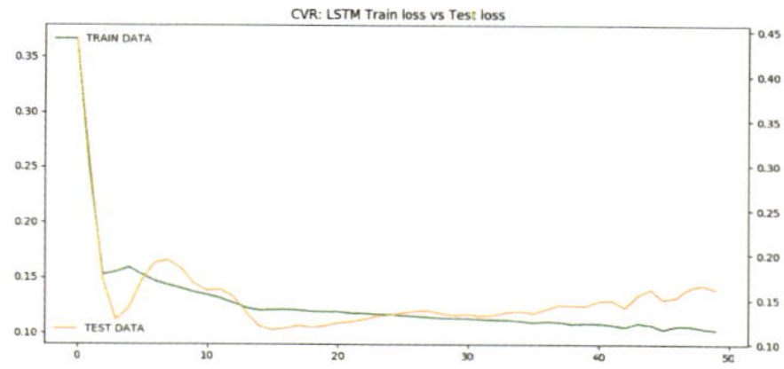

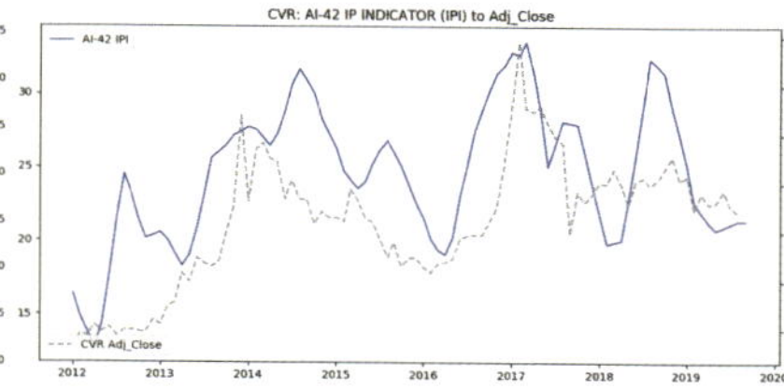

DBD

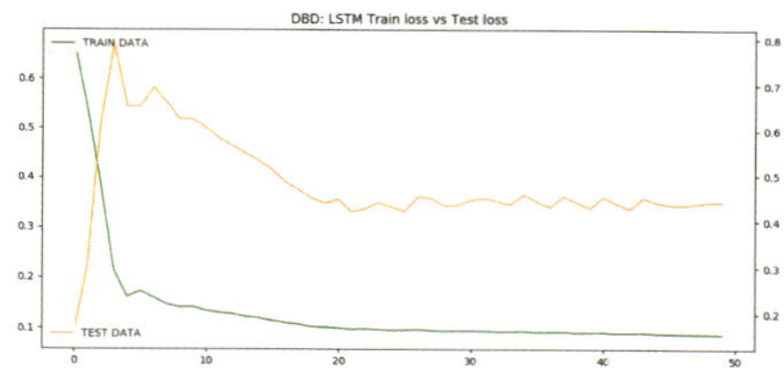

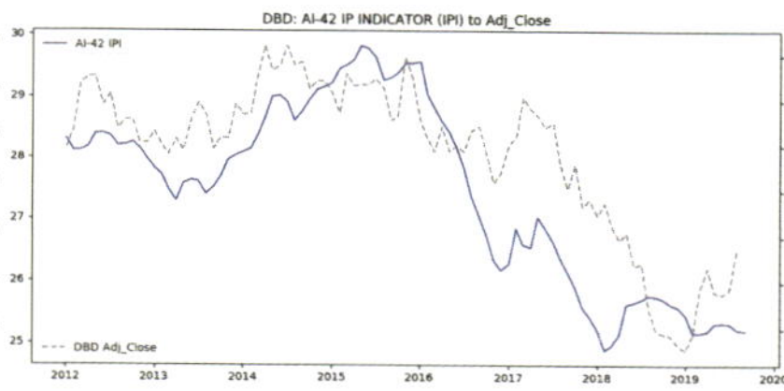

CGNX

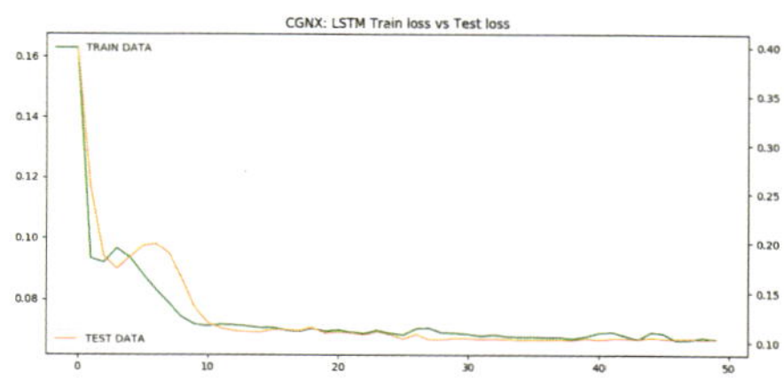

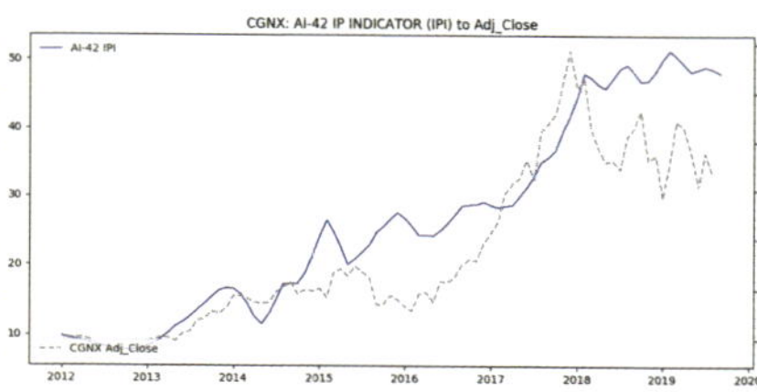

MIME

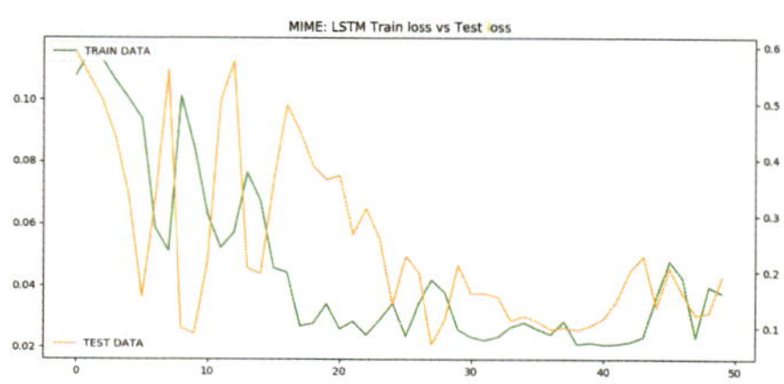

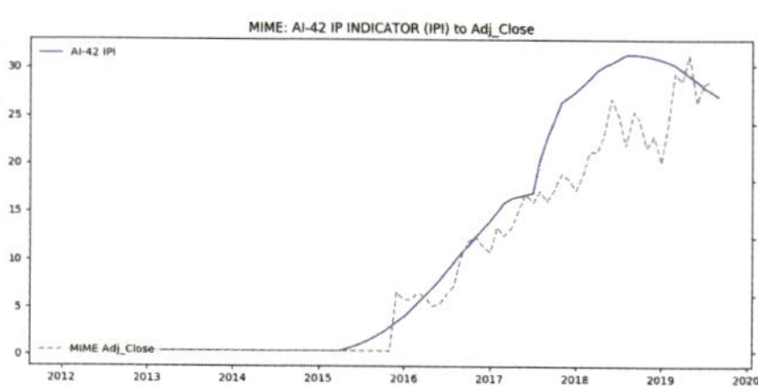

IDXX

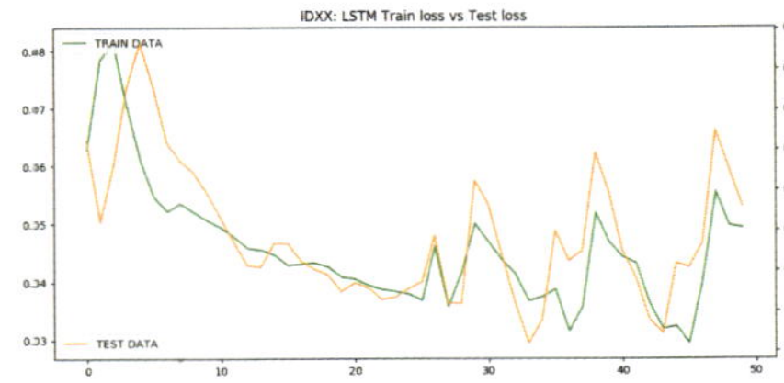

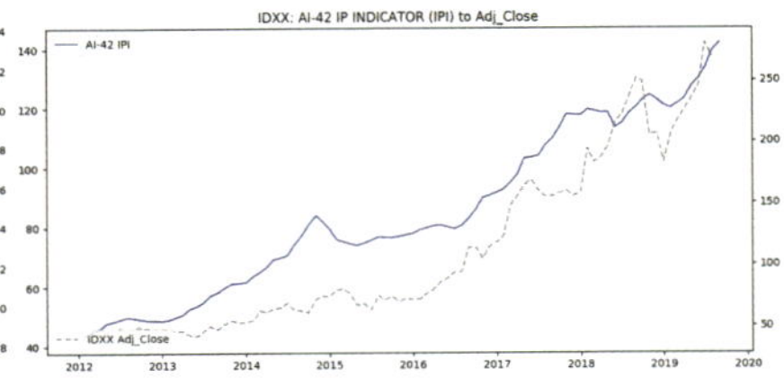

WD

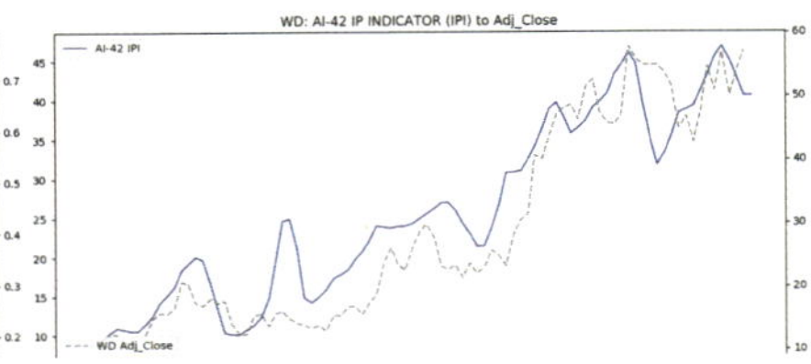

EIGI

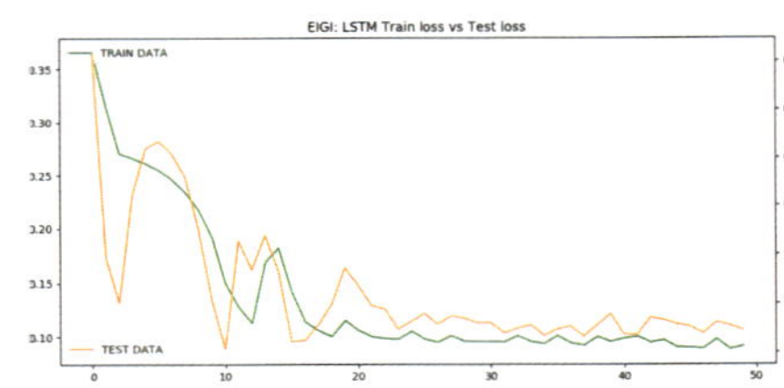

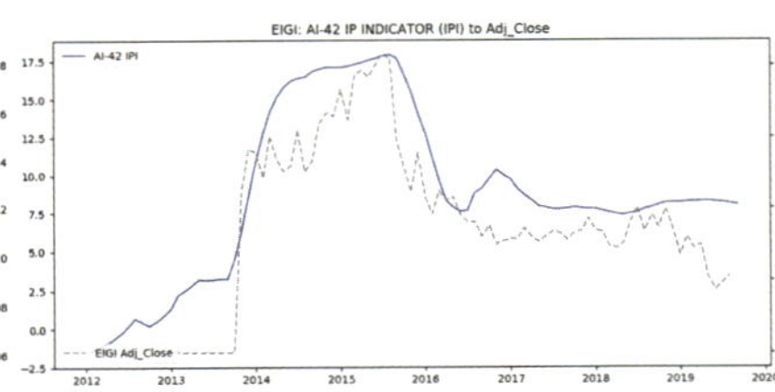

VSAT

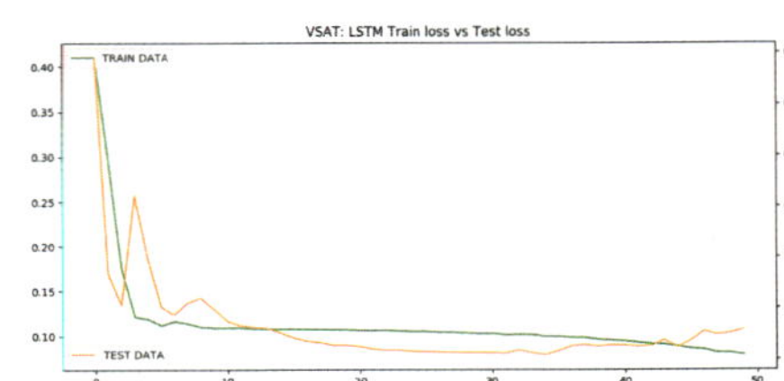

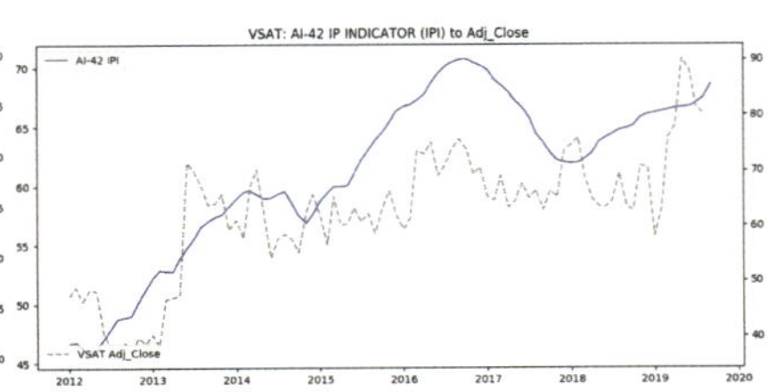

WHR

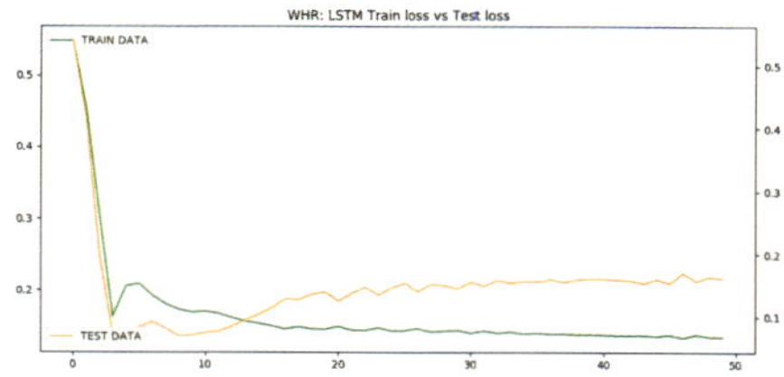

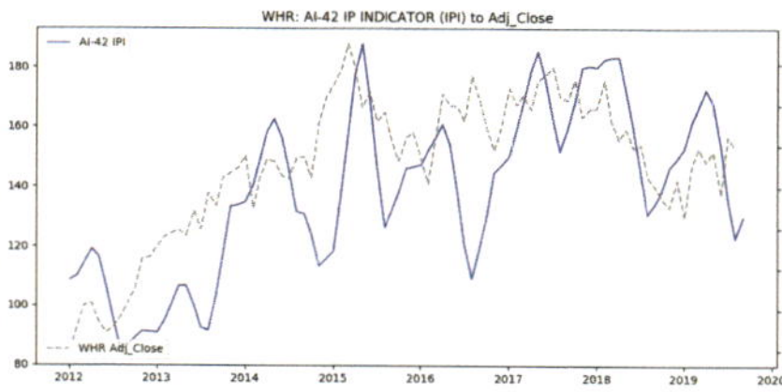

NVTR

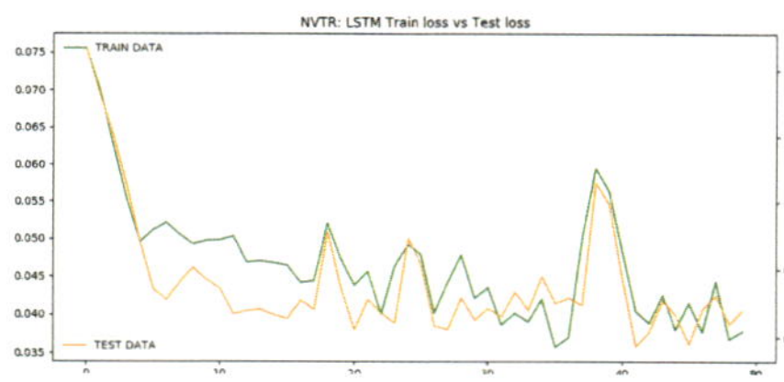

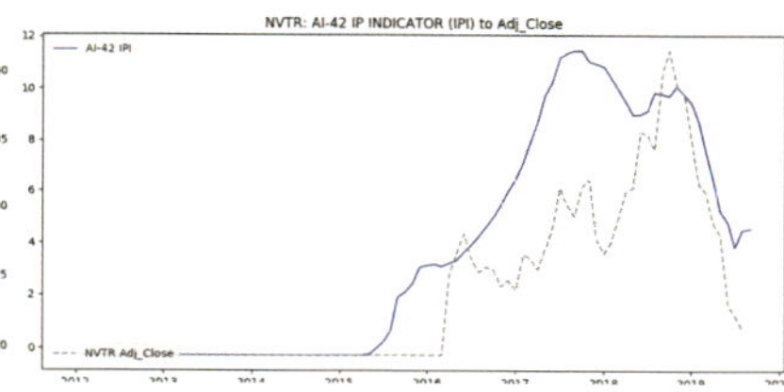

NTRA

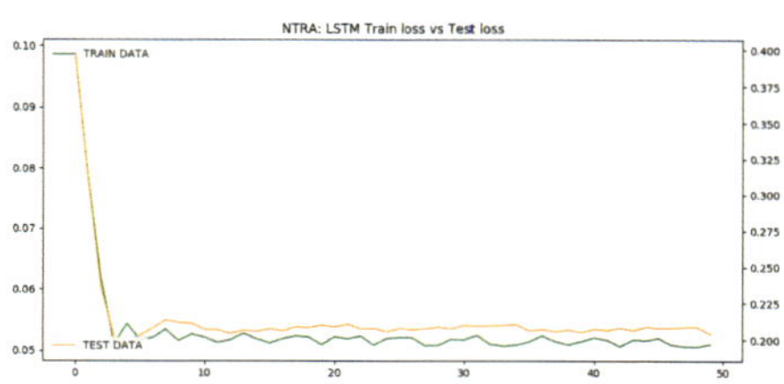

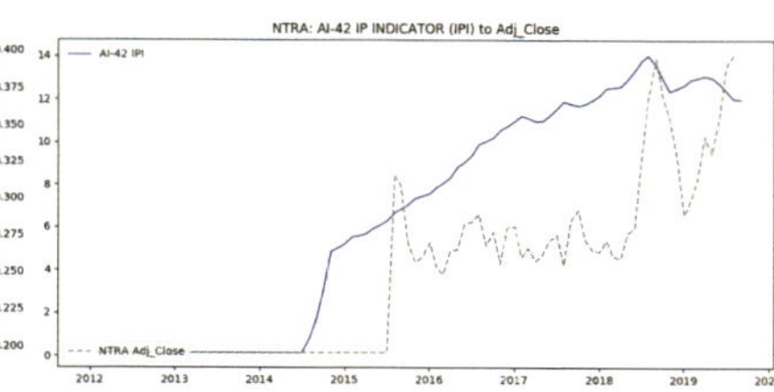

CATC

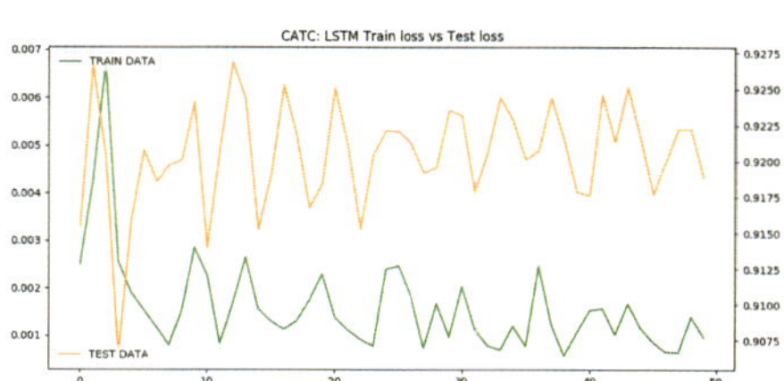

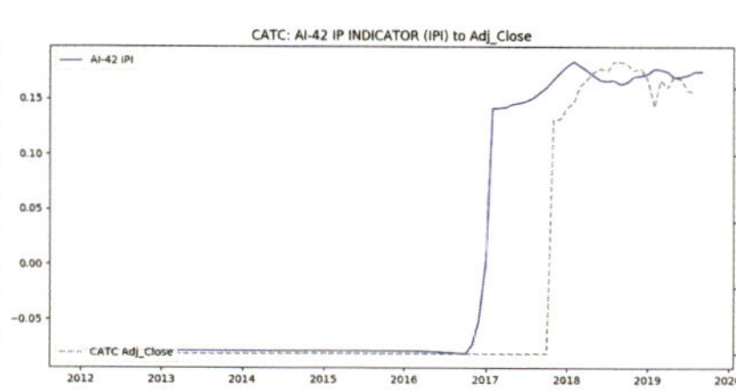

TWLO

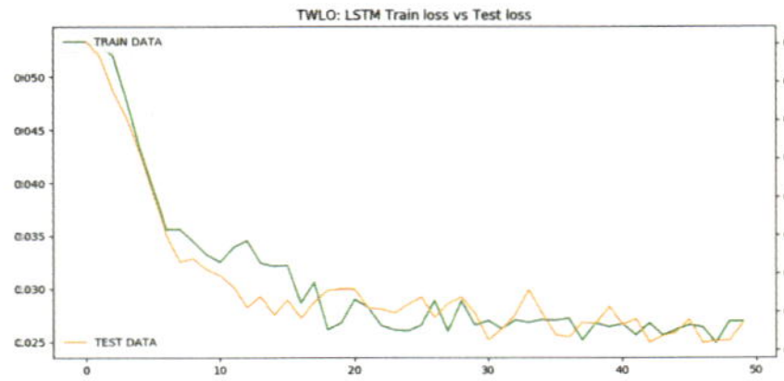

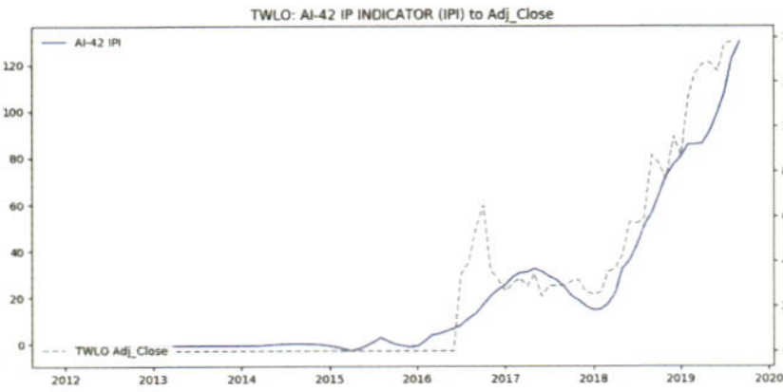

NTAP

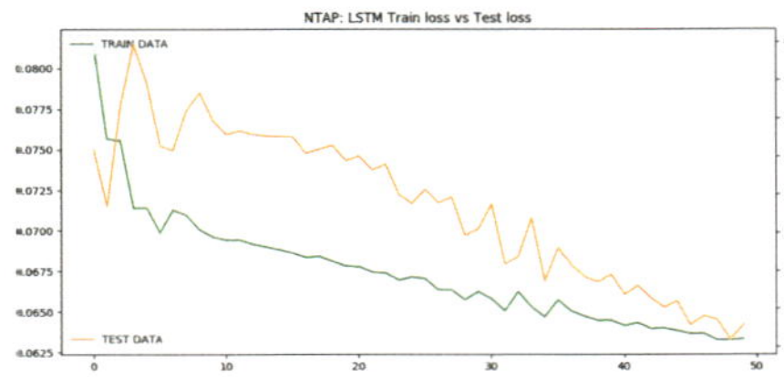

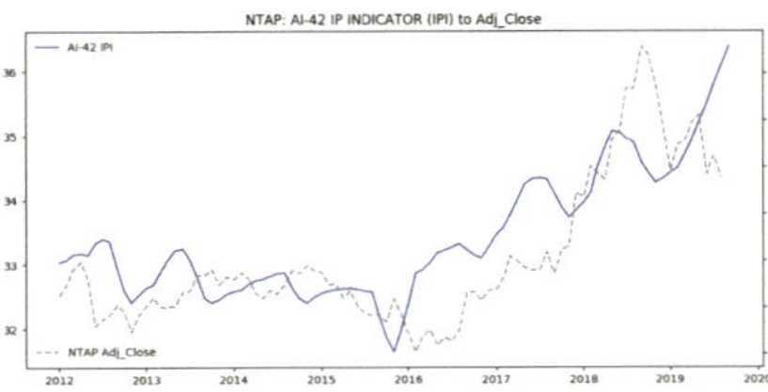

HOLX

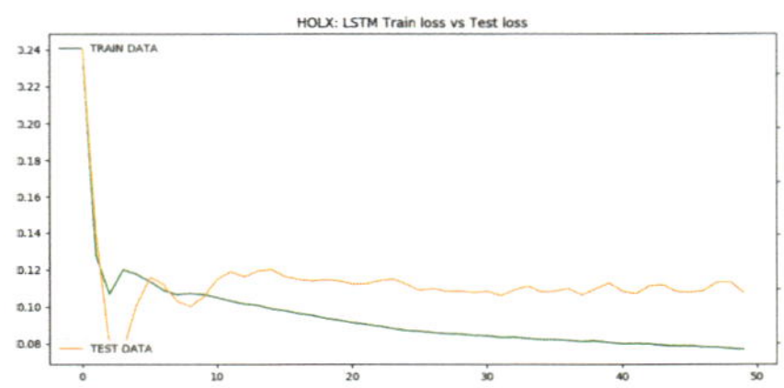

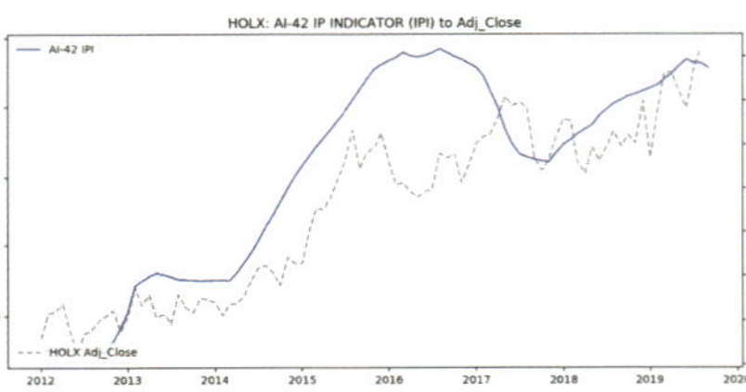

ISRG

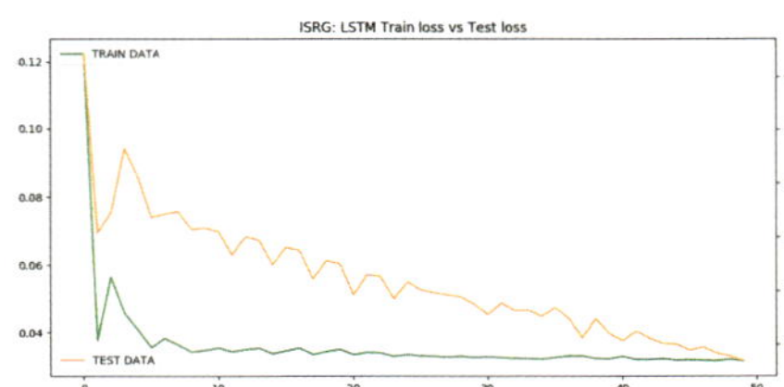

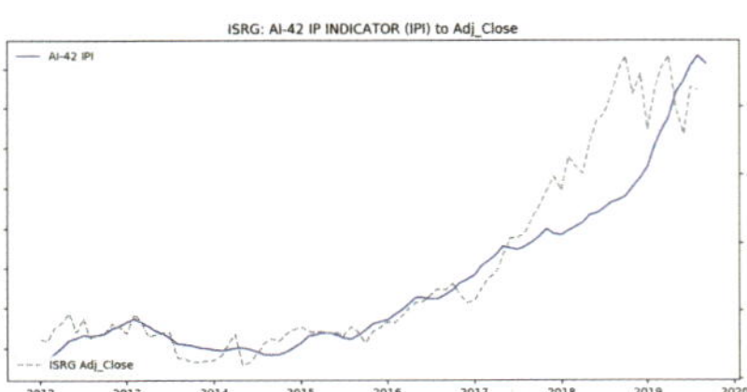

GT

GT: LSTM Train loss vs Test loss
TRAIN DATA
TEST DATA

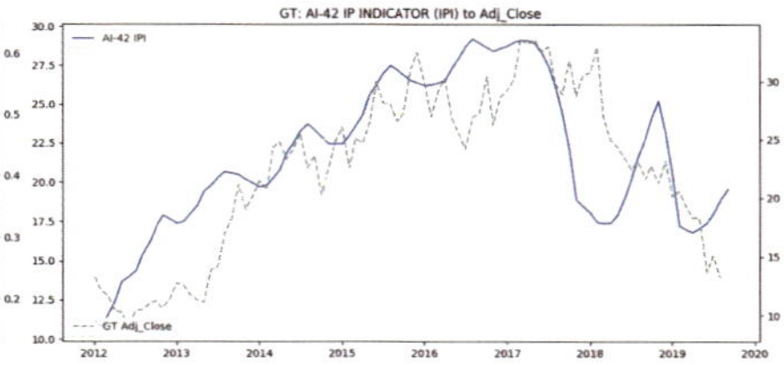
GT: AI-42 IP INDICATOR (IPI) to Adj_Close
AI-42 IPI
GT Adj_Close

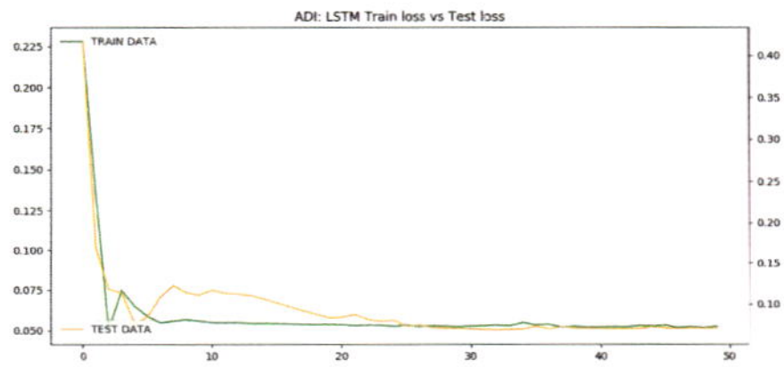
ADI: LSTM Train loss vs Test loss
TRAIN DATA
TEST DATA

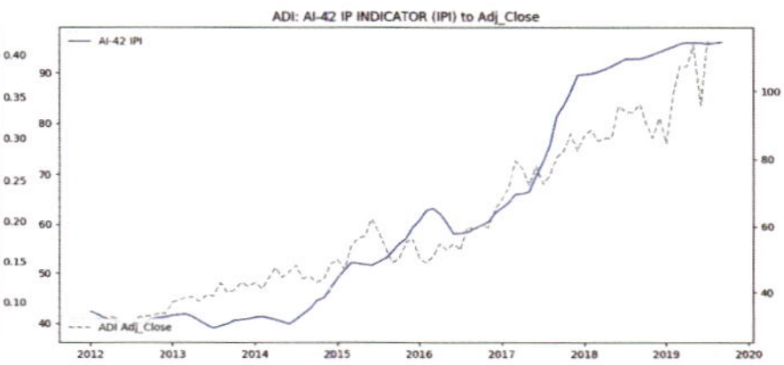
ADI: AI-42 IP INDICATOR (IPI) to Adj_Close
AI-42 IPI
ADI Adj_Close

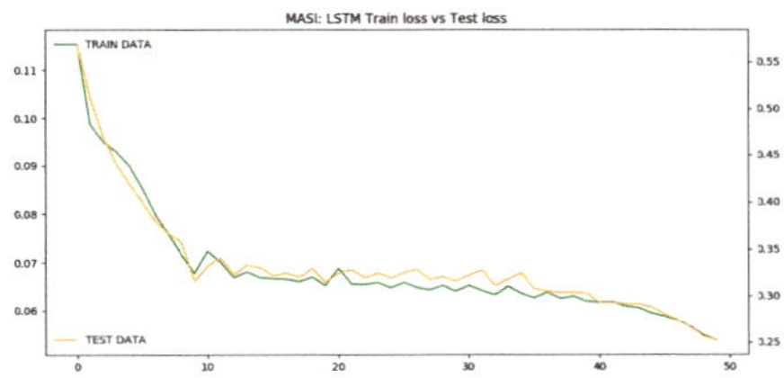
MASI: LSTM Train loss vs Test loss
TRAIN DATA
TEST DATA

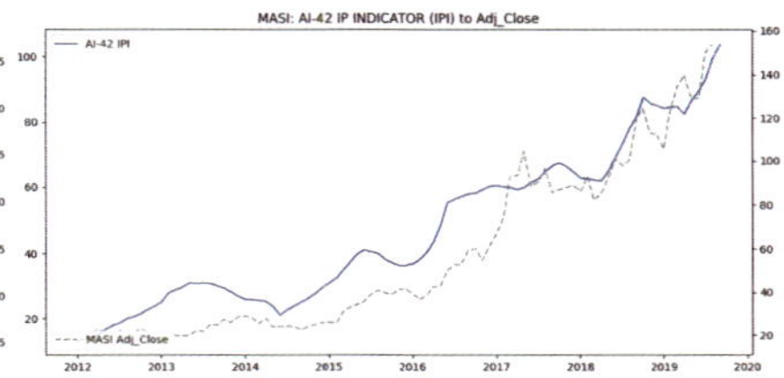
MASI: AI-42 IP INDICATOR (IPI) to Adj_Close
AI-42 IPI
MASI Adj_Close

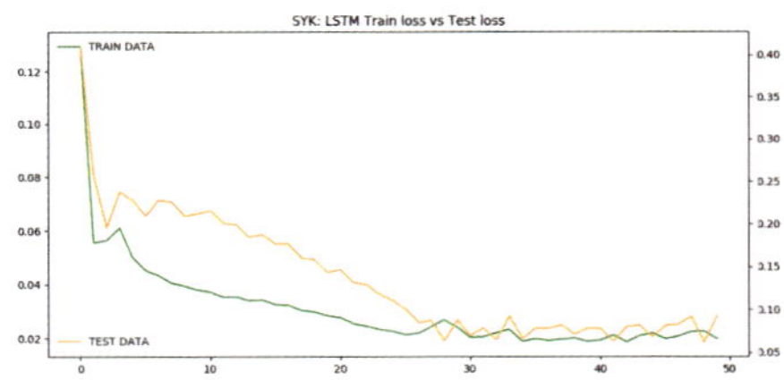
SYK: LSTM Train loss vs Test loss
TRAIN DATA
TEST DATA

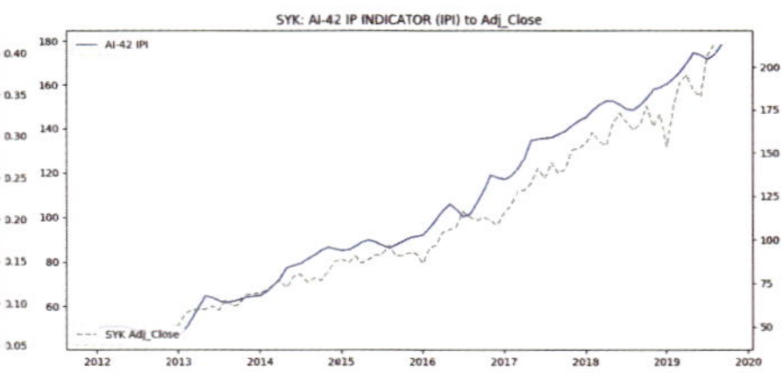
SYK: AI-42 IP INDICATOR (IPI) to Adj_Close
AI-42 IPI
SYK Adj_Close

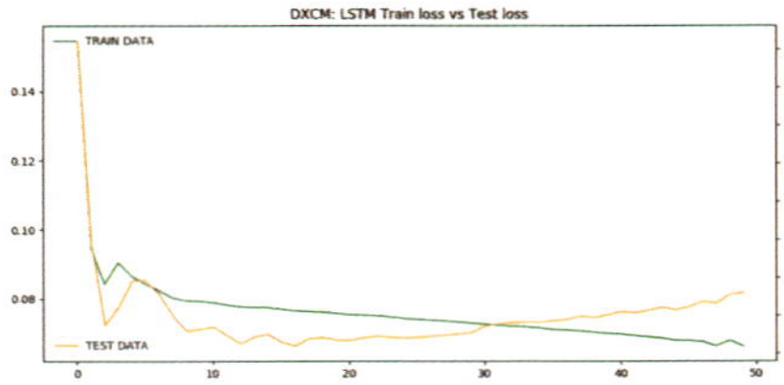
DXCM: LSTM Train loss vs Test loss
TRAIN DATA
TEST DATA

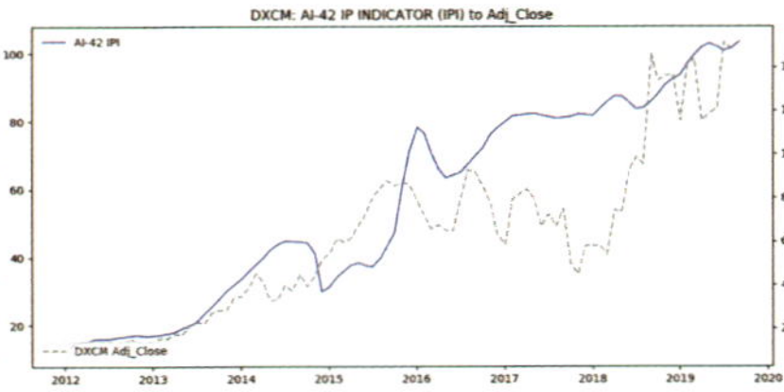
DXCM: AI-42 IP INDICATOR (IPI) to Adj_Close
AI-42 IPI
DXCM Adj_Close

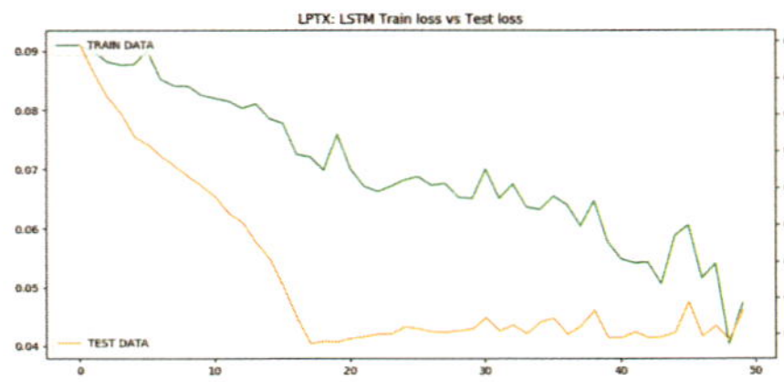
LPTX: LSTM Train loss vs Test loss
TRAIN DATA
TEST DATA

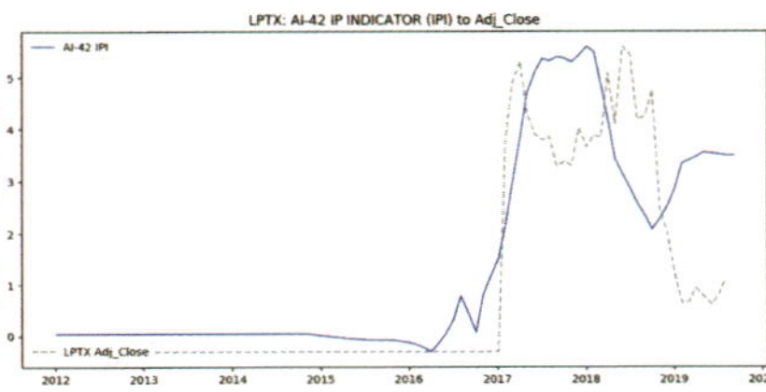
LPTX: AI-42 IP INDICATOR (IPI) to Adj_Close
AI-42 IPI
LPTX Adj_Close

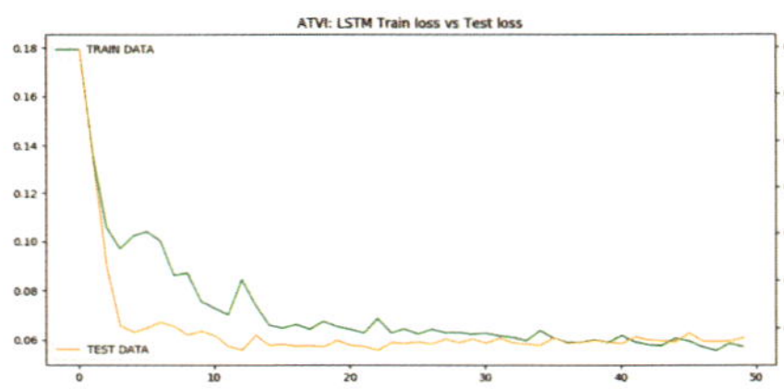
ATVI: LSTM Train loss vs Test loss
TRAIN DATA
TEST DATA

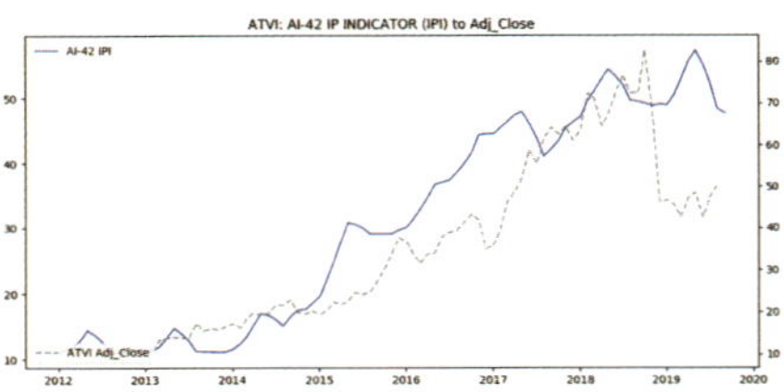
ATVI: AI-42 IP INDICATOR (IPI) to Adj_Close
AI-42 IPI
ATVI Adj_Close

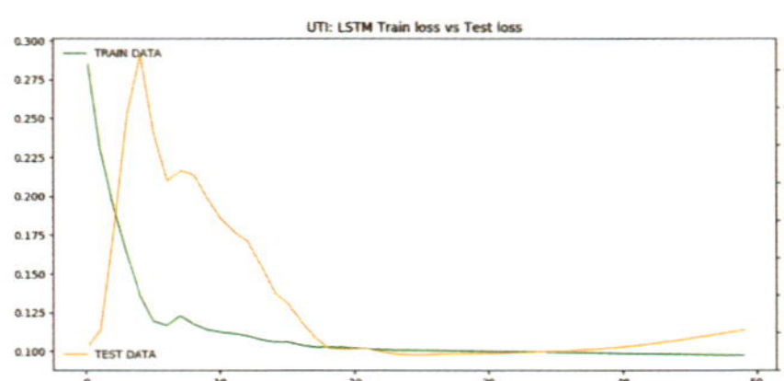
UTI: LSTM Train loss vs Test loss
TRAIN DATA
TEST DATA

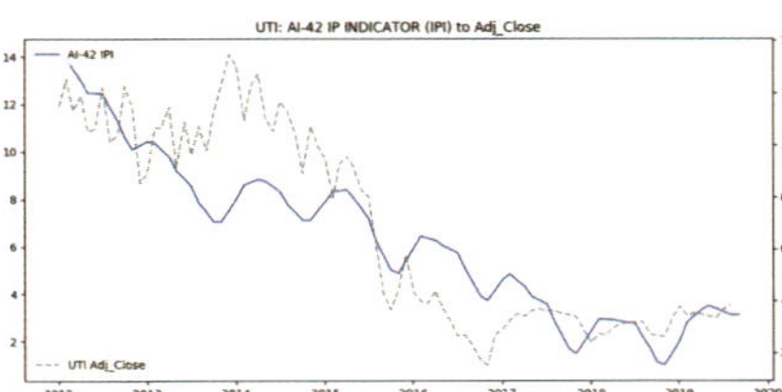
UTI: AI-42 IP INDICATOR (IPI) to Adj_Close
AI-42 IPI
UTI Adj_Close

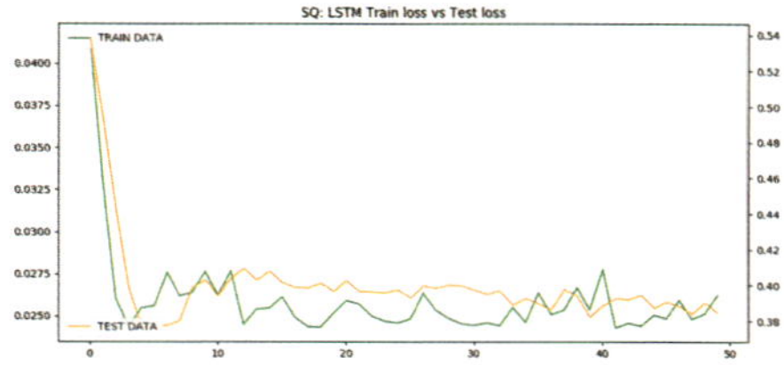
SQ: LSTM Train loss vs Test loss
TRAIN DATA
TEST DATA

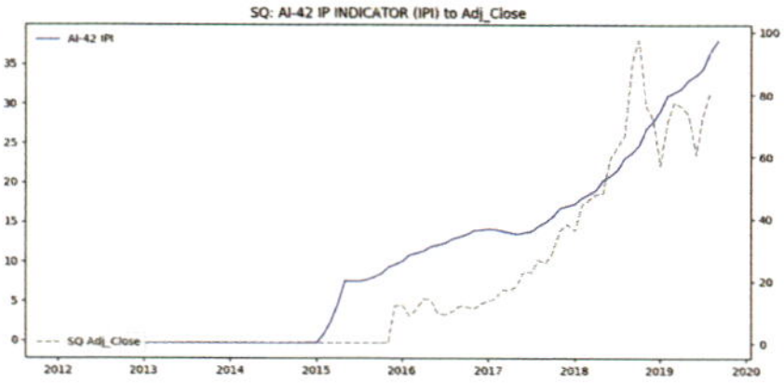
SQ: AI-42 IP INDICATOR (IPI) to Adj_Close
AI-42 IPI
SQ Adj_Close

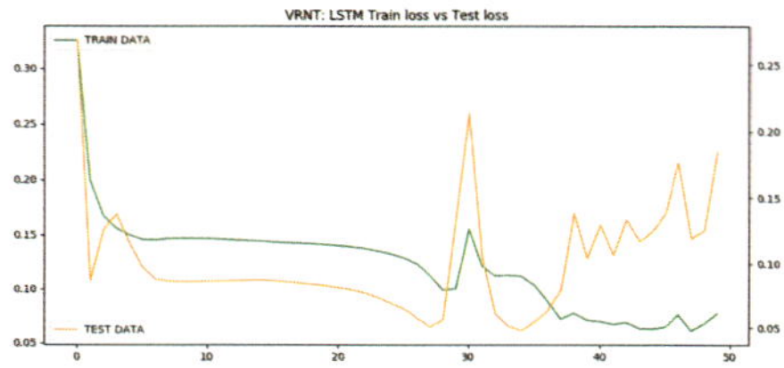
VRNT: LSTM Train loss vs Test loss
TRAIN DATA
TEST DATA

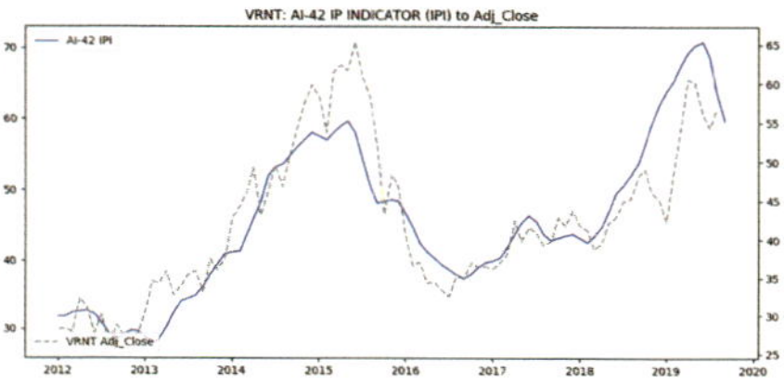
VRNT: AI-42 IP INDICATOR (IPI) to Adj_Close
AI-42 IPI
VRNT Adj_Close

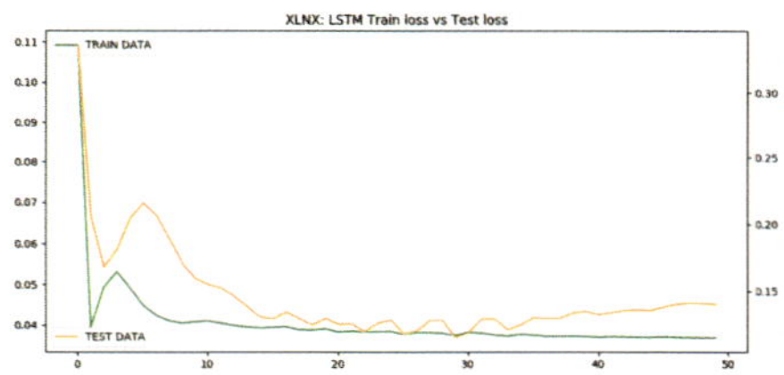
XLNX: LSTM Train loss vs Test loss
TRAIN DATA
TEST DATA

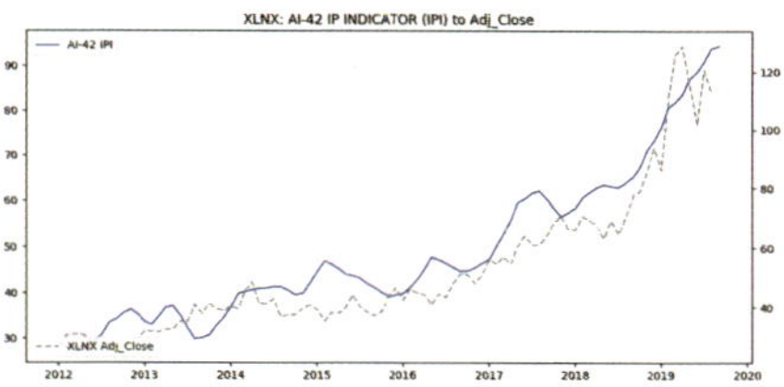
XLNX: AI-42 IP INDICATOR (IPI) to Adj_Close
AI-42 IPI
XLNX Adj_Close

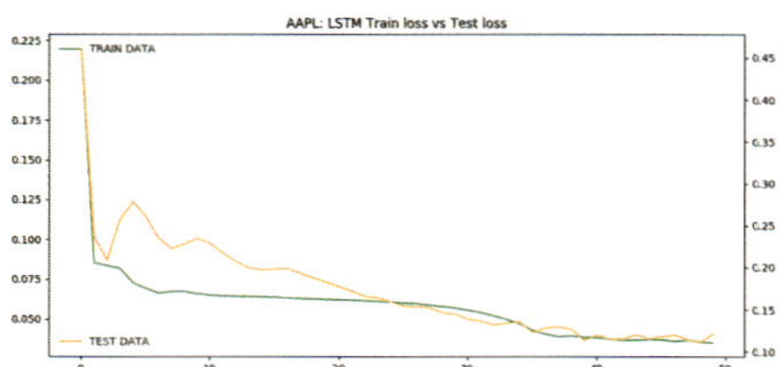
AAPL: LSTM Train loss vs Test loss
TRAIN DATA
TEST DATA

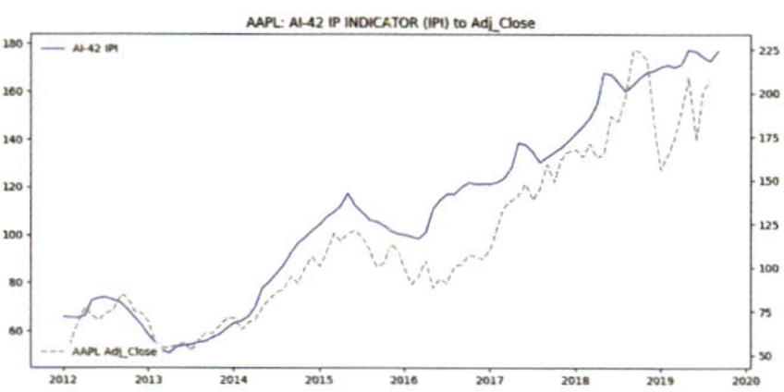
AAPL: AI-42 IP INDICATOR (IPI) to Adj_Close
AI-42 IPI
AAPL Adj_Close

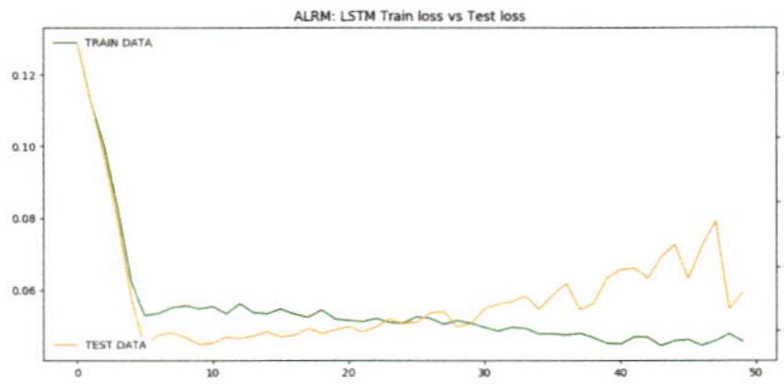
ALRM: LSTM Train loss vs Test loss
TRAIN DATA
TEST DATA

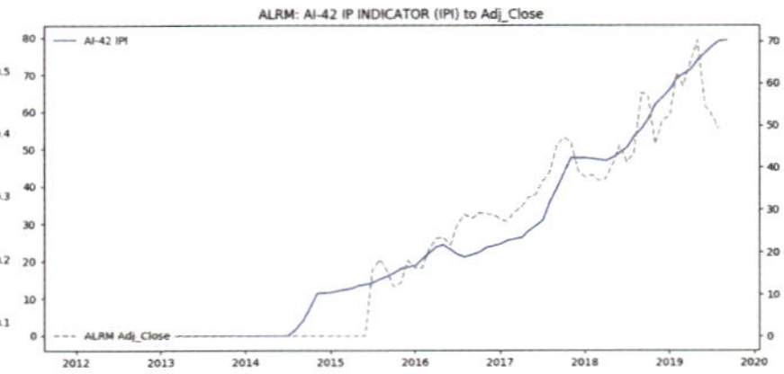
ALRM: AI-42 IP INDICATOR (IPI) to Adj_Close
AI-42 IPI
ALRM Adj_Close

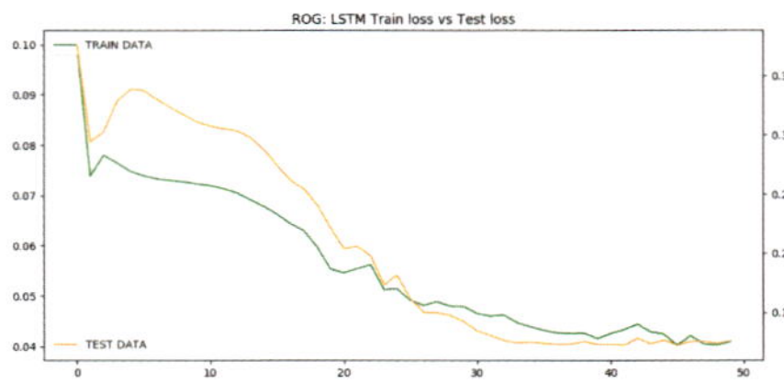
ROG: LSTM Train loss vs Test loss
TRAIN DATA
TEST DATA

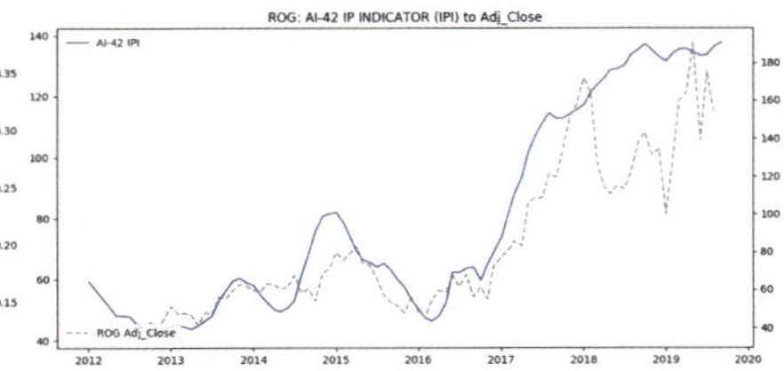
ROG: AI-42 IP INDICATOR (IPI) to Adj_Close
AI-42 IPI
ROG Adj_Close

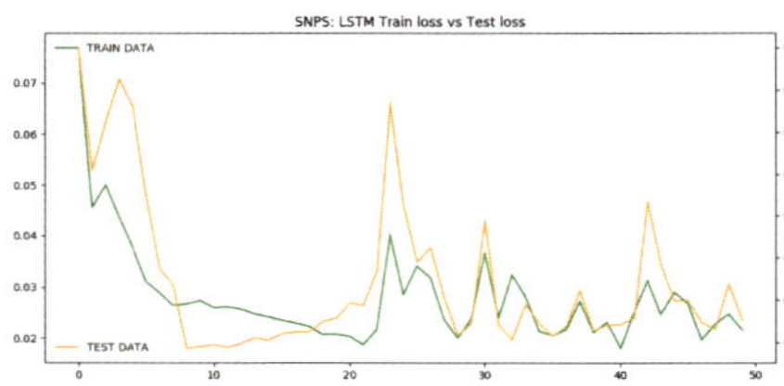
SNPS: LSTM Train loss vs Test loss
TRAIN DATA
TEST DATA

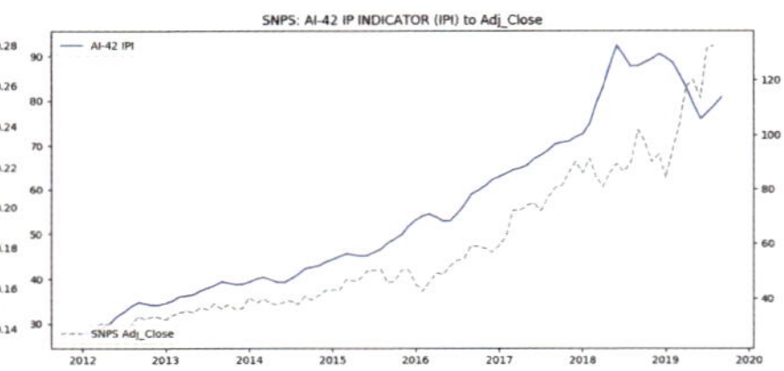
SNPS: AI-42 IP INDICATOR (IPI) to Adj_Close
AI-42 IPI
SNPS Adj_Close

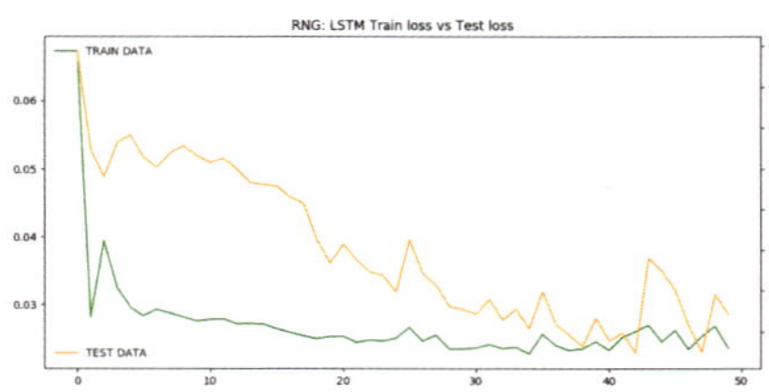
RNG: LSTM Train loss vs Test loss
TRAIN DATA
TEST DATA

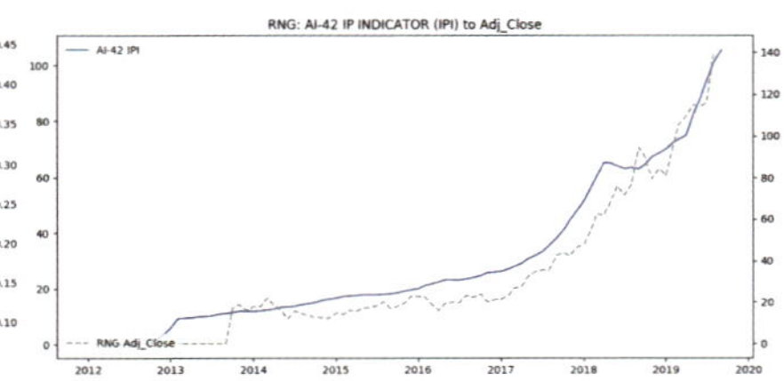
RNG: AI-42 IP INDICATOR (IPI) to Adj_Close
AI-42 IPI
RNG Adj_Close

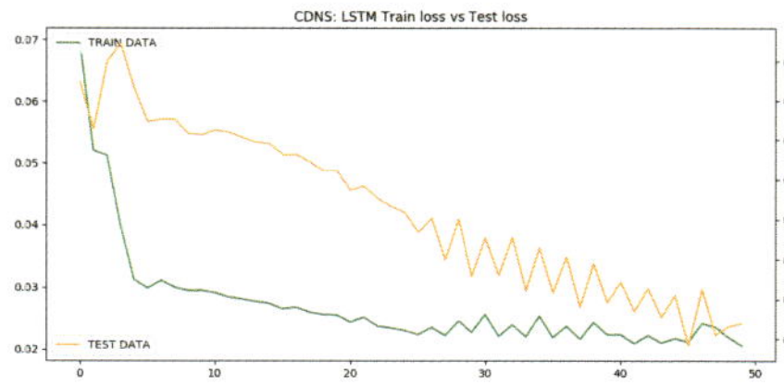
CDNS: LSTM Train loss vs Test loss
TRAIN DATA
TEST DATA

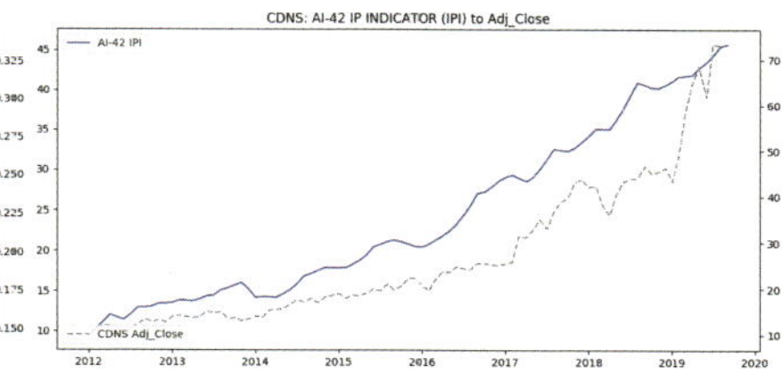
CDNS: AI-42 IP INDICATOR (IPI) to Adj_Close
AI-42 IPI
CDNS Adj_Close

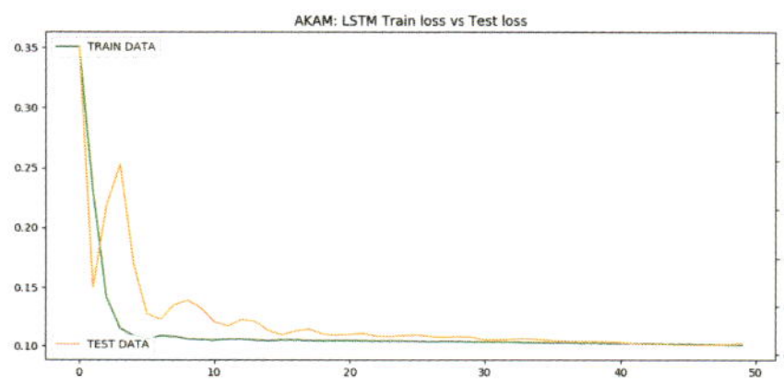
AKAM: LSTM Train loss vs Test loss
TRAIN DATA
TEST DATA

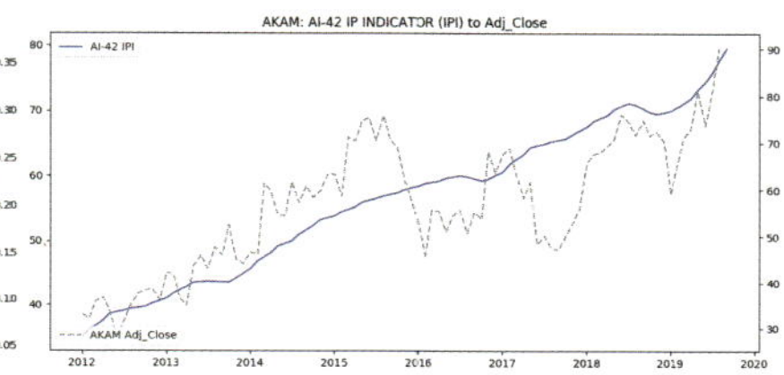
AKAM: AI-42 IP INDICATOR (IPI) to Adj_Close
AI-42 IPI
AKAM Adj_Close

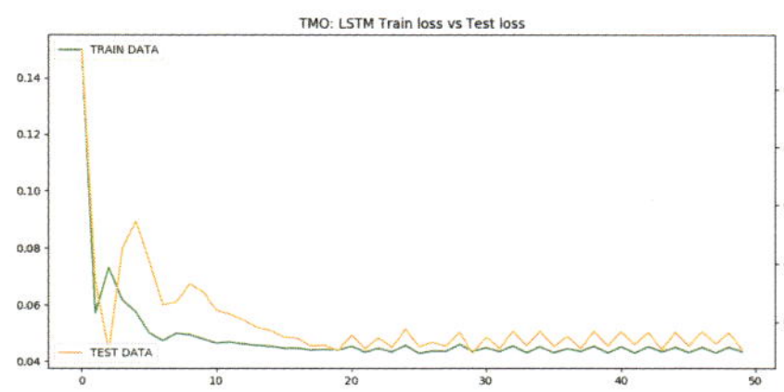
TMO: LSTM Train loss vs Test loss
TRAIN DATA
TEST DATA

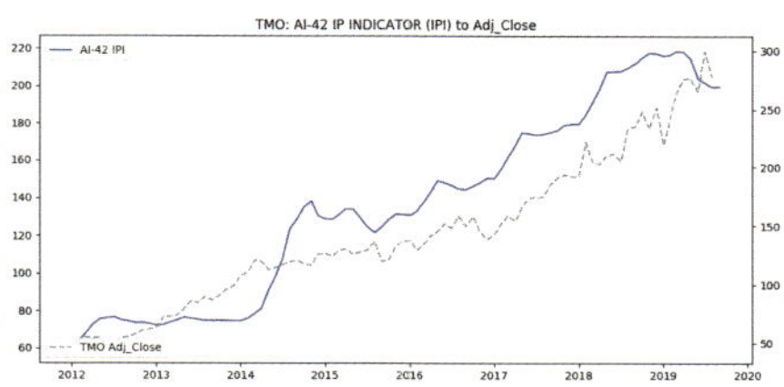
TMO: AI-42 IP INDICATOR (IPI) to Adj_Close
AI-42 IPI
TMO Adj_Close

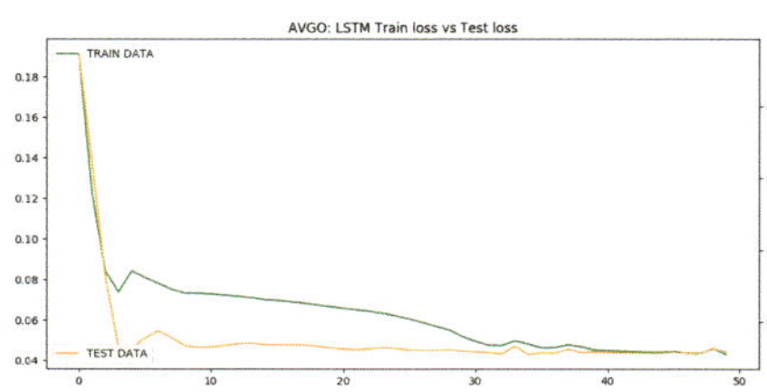
AVGO: LSTM Train loss vs Test loss
TRAIN DATA
TEST DATA

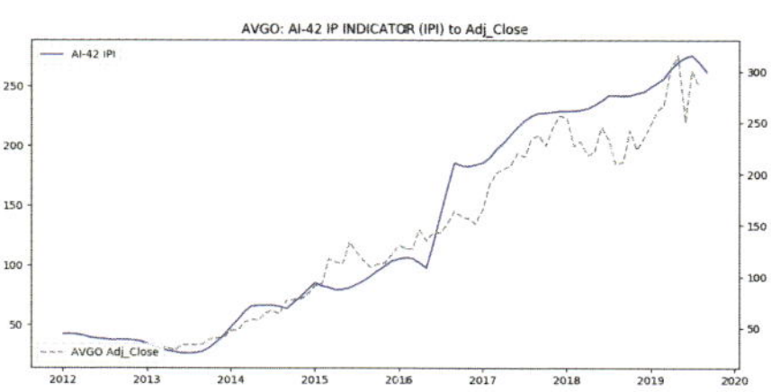
AVGO: AI-42 IP INDICATOR (IPI) to Adj_Close
AI-42 IPI
AVGO Adj_Close

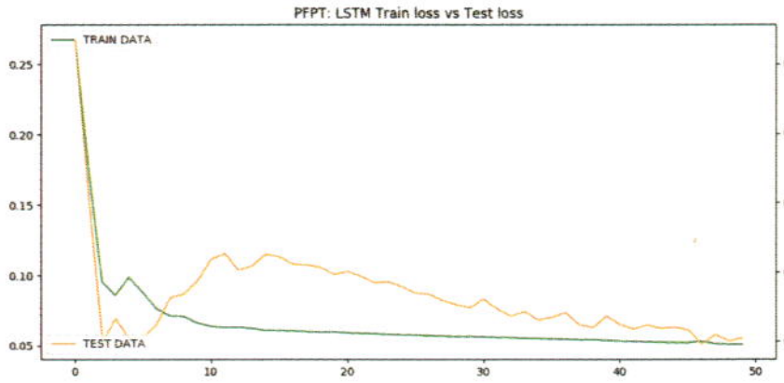
PFPT: LSTM Train loss vs Test loss
TRAIN DATA
TEST DATA

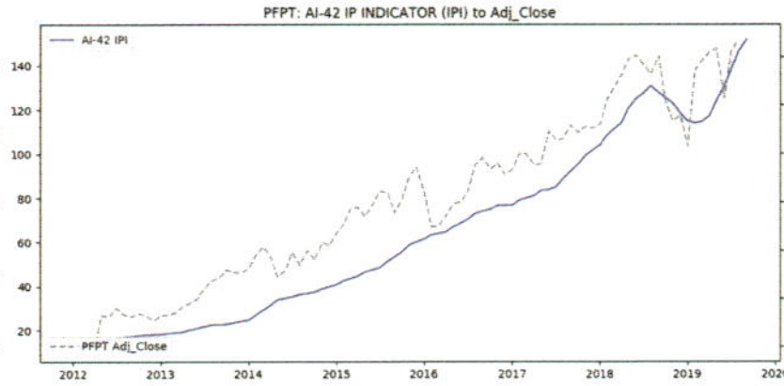
PFPT: AI-42 IP INDICATOR (IPI) to Adj_Close
AI-42 IPI
PFPT Adj_Close

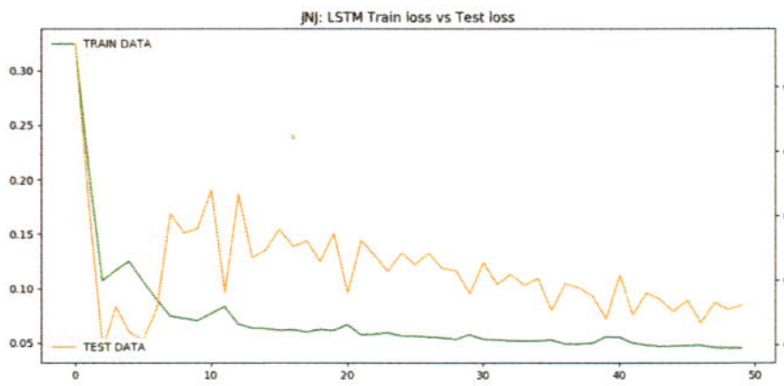
JNJ: LSTM Train loss vs Test loss
TRAIN DATA
TEST DATA

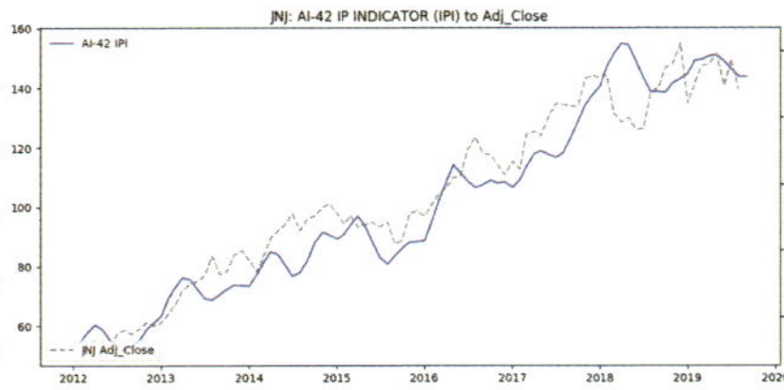
JNJ: AI-42 IP INDICATOR (IPI) to Adj_Close
AI-42 IPI
JNJ Adj_Close

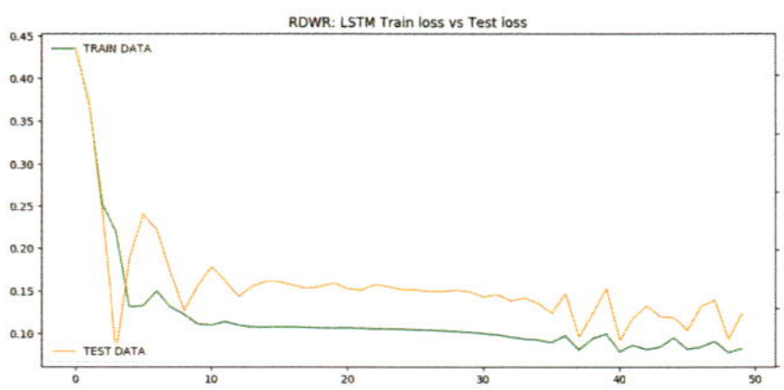
RDWR: LSTM Train loss vs Test loss
TRAIN DATA
TEST DATA

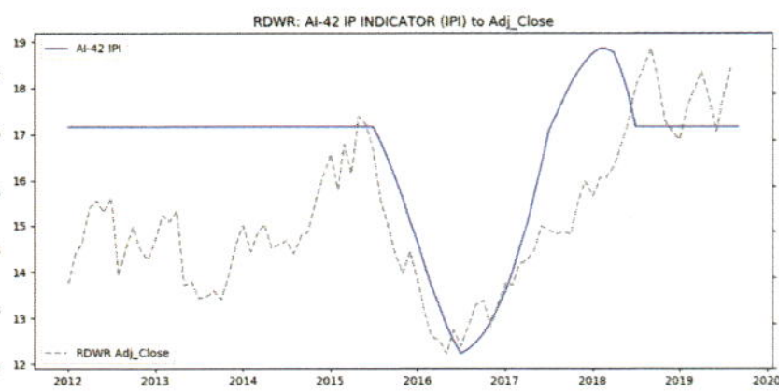
RDWR: AI-42 IP INDICATOR (IPI) to Adj_Close
AI-42 IPI
RDWR Adj_Close

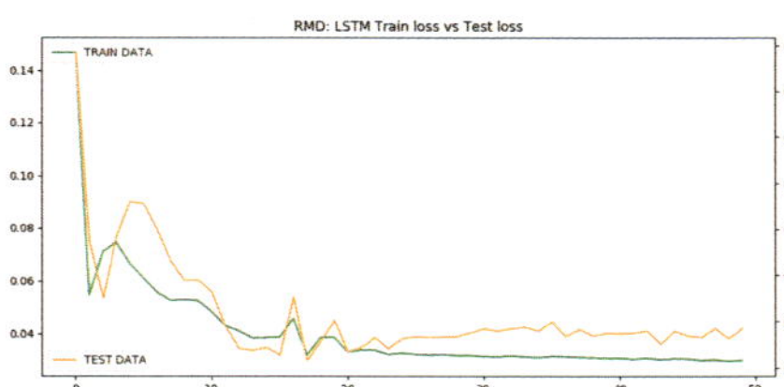
RMD: LSTM Train loss vs Test loss
TRAIN DATA
TEST DATA

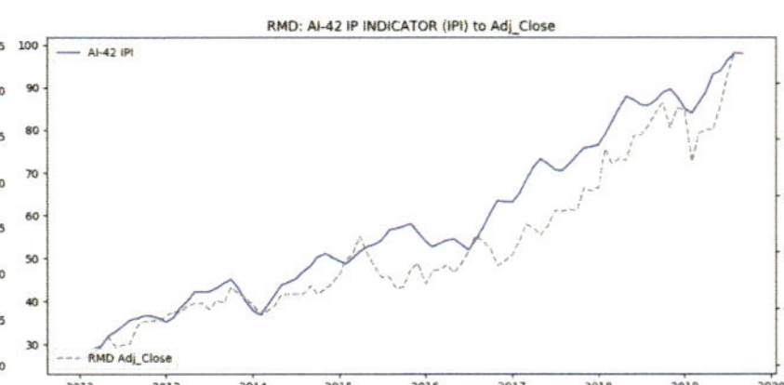
RMD: AI-42 IP INDICATOR (IPI) to Adj_Close
AI-42 IPI
RMD Adj_Close

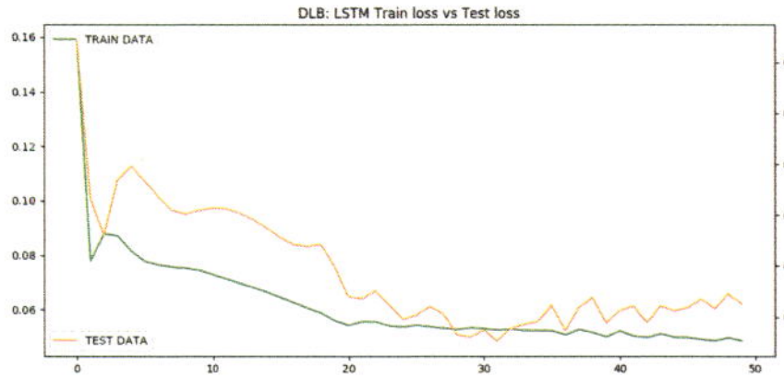
DLB: LSTM Train loss vs Test loss
TRAIN DATA
TEST DATA

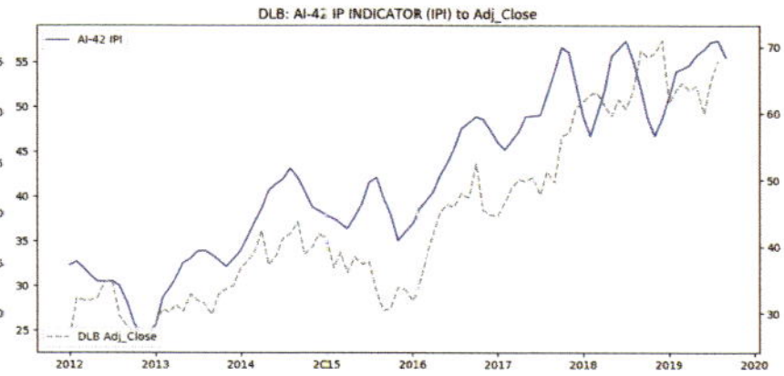
DLB: AI-42 IP INDICATOR (IPI) to Adj_Close
AI-42 IPI
DLB Adj_Close

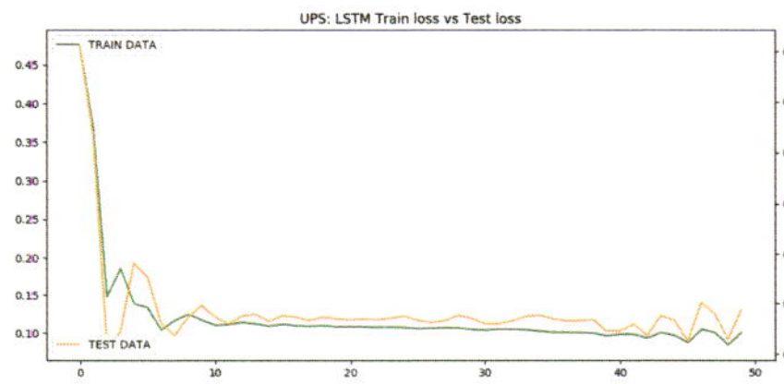
UPS: LSTM Train loss vs Test loss
TRAIN DATA
TEST DATA

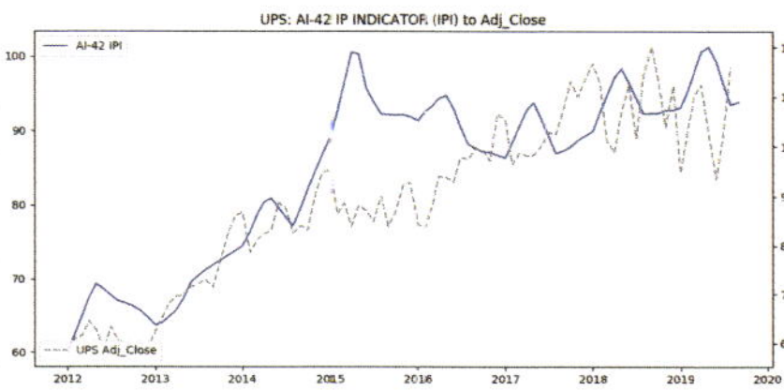
UPS: AI-42 IP INDICATOR (IPI) to Adj_Close
AI-42 IPI
UPS Adj_Close

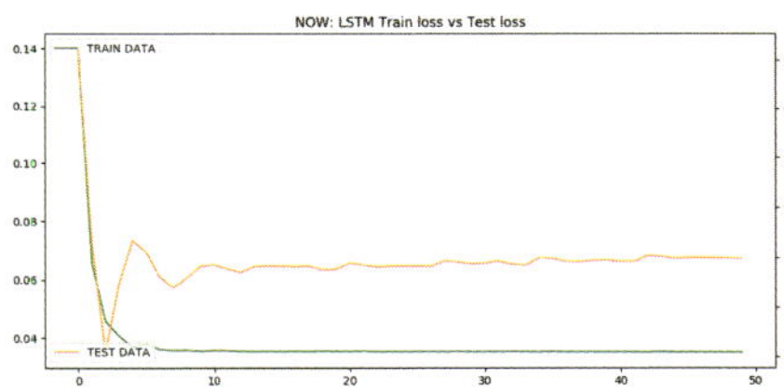
NOW: LSTM Train loss vs Test loss
TRAIN DATA
TEST DATA

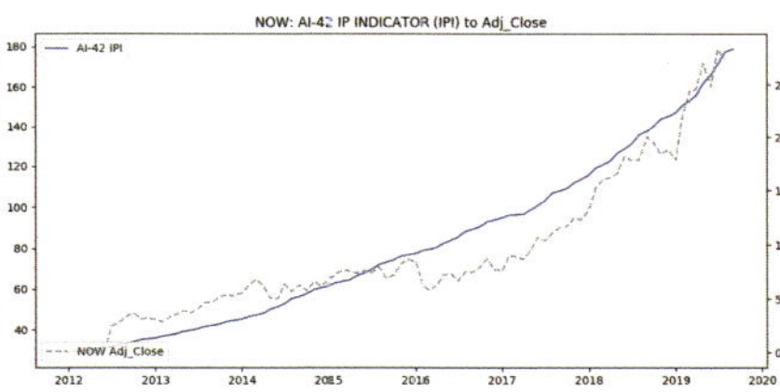
NOW: AI-42 IP INDICATOR (IPI) to Adj_Close
AI-42 IPI
NOW Adj_Close

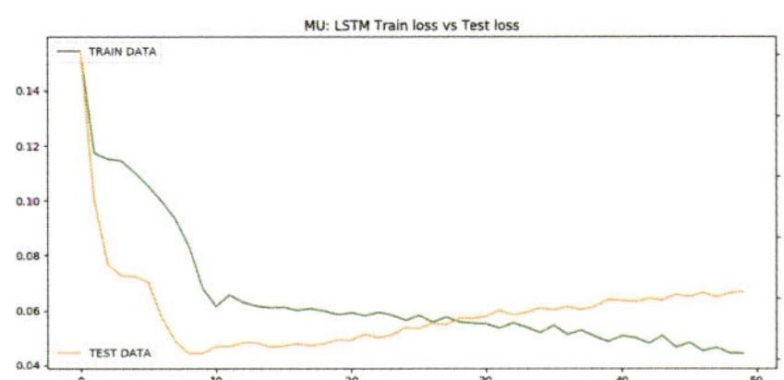
MU: LSTM Train loss vs Test loss
TRAIN DATA
TEST DATA

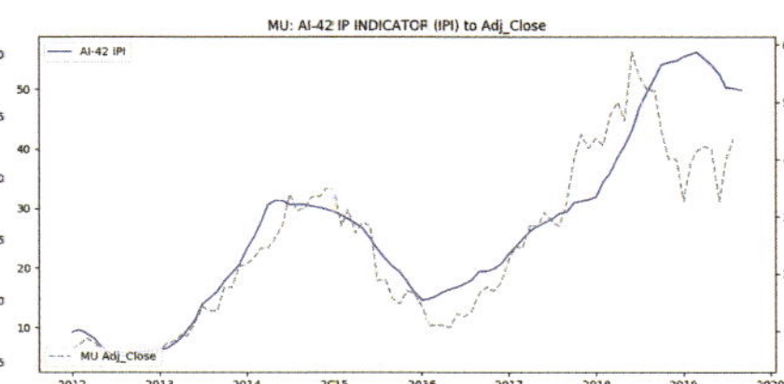
MU: AI-42 IP INDICATOR (IPI) to Adj_Close
AI-42 IPI
MU Adj_Close

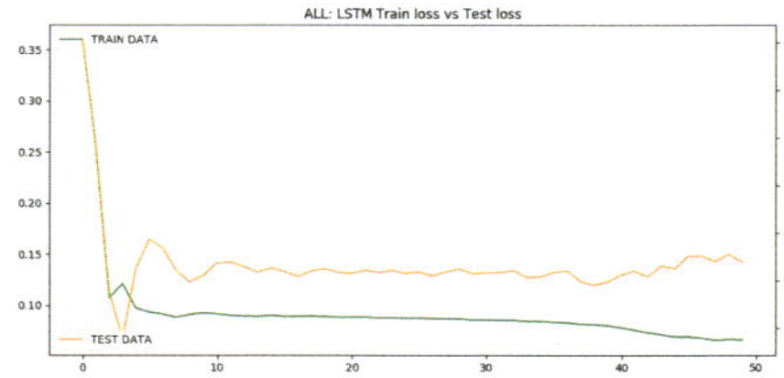
ALL: LSTM Train loss vs Test loss
TRAIN DATA
TEST DATA

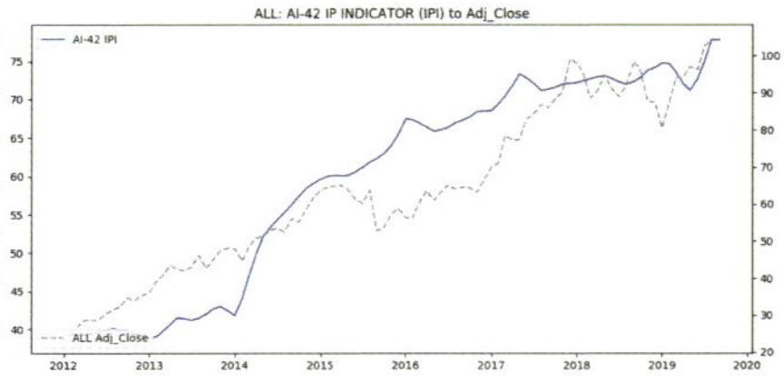
ALL: AI-42 IP INDICATOR (IPI) to Adj_Close
AI-42 IPI
ALL Adj_Close

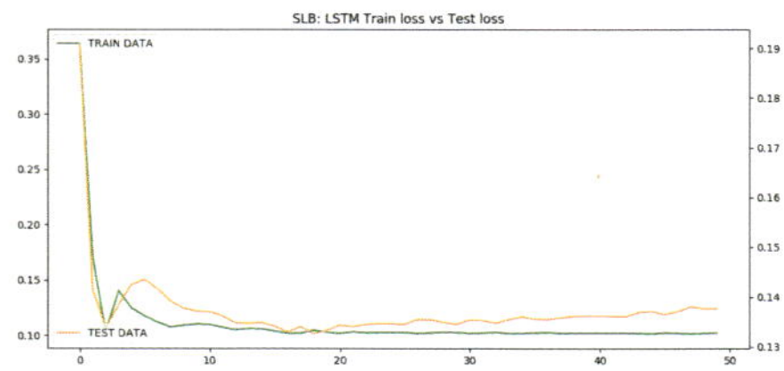
SLB: LSTM Train loss vs Test loss
TRAIN DATA
TEST DATA

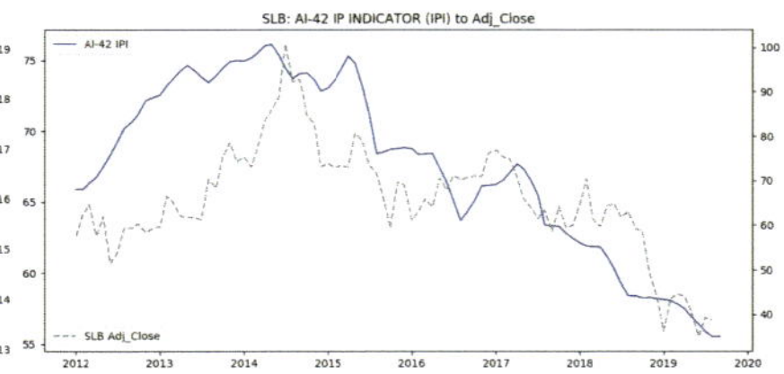
SLB: AI-42 IP INDICATOR (IPI) to Adj_Close
AI-42 IPI
SLB Adj_Close

MA: LSTM Train loss vs Test loss
TRAIN DATA
TEST DATA

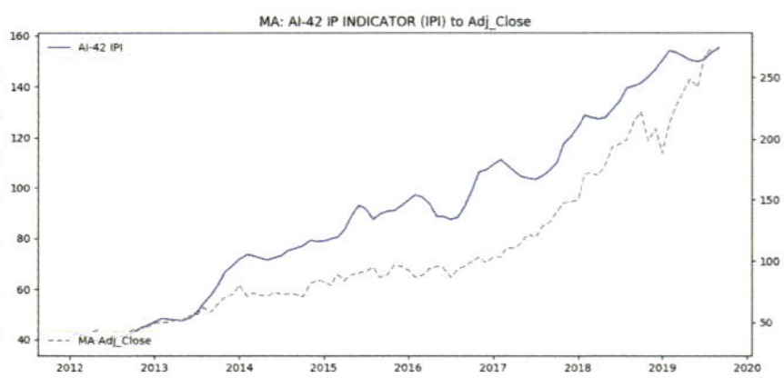
MA: AI-42 IP INDICATOR (IPI) to Adj_Close
AI-42 IPI
MA Adj_Close

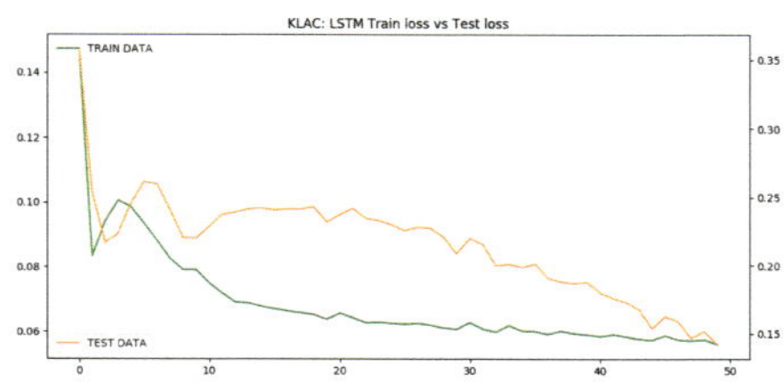
KLAC: LSTM Train loss vs Test loss
TRAIN DATA
TEST DATA

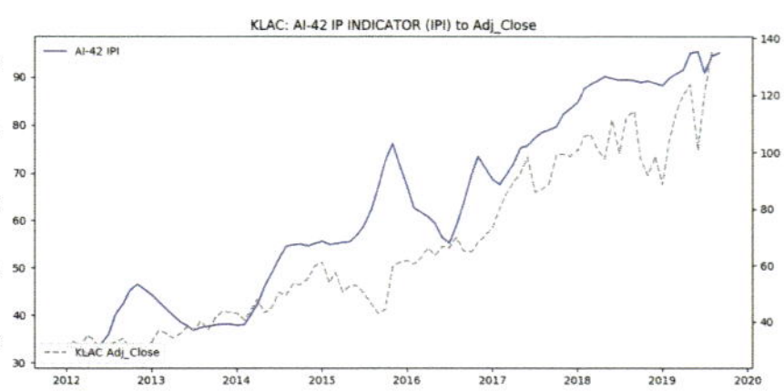
KLAC: AI-42 IP INDICATOR (IPI) to Adj_Close
AI-42 IPI
KLAC Adj_Close

ZNGA: LSTM Train loss vs Test loss
TRAIN DATA
TEST DATA

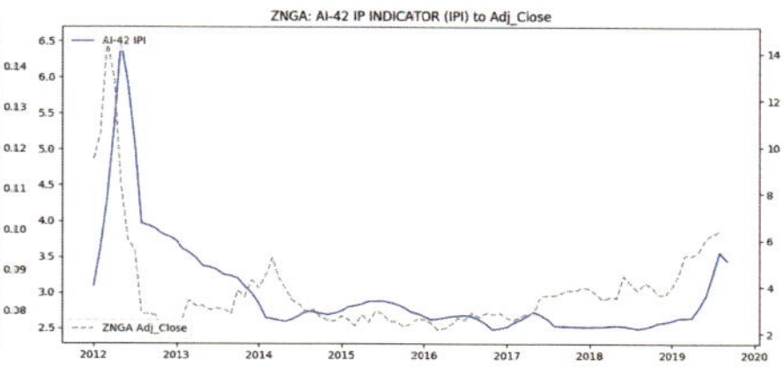
ZNGA: AI-42 IP INDICATOR (IPI) to Adj_Close
AI-42 IPI
ZNGA Adj_Close

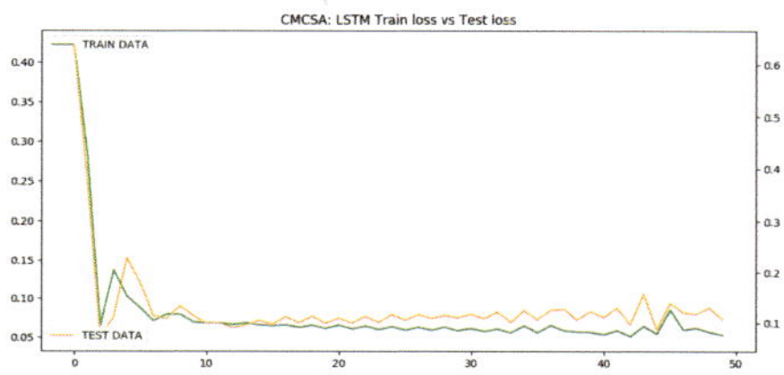
CMCSA: LSTM Train loss vs Test loss
TRAIN DATA
TEST DATA

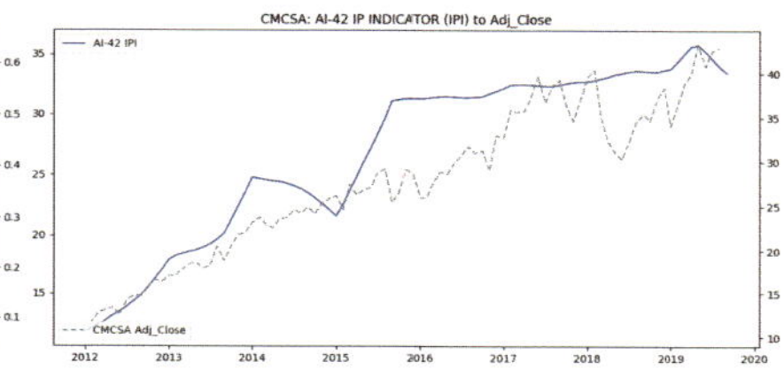
CMCSA: AI-42 IP INDICATOR (IPI) to Adj_Close
AI-42 IPI
CMCSA Adj_Close

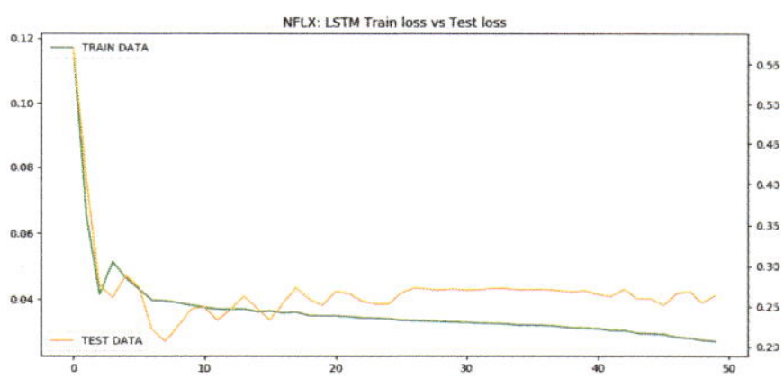
NFLX: LSTM Train loss vs Test loss
TRAIN DATA
TEST DATA

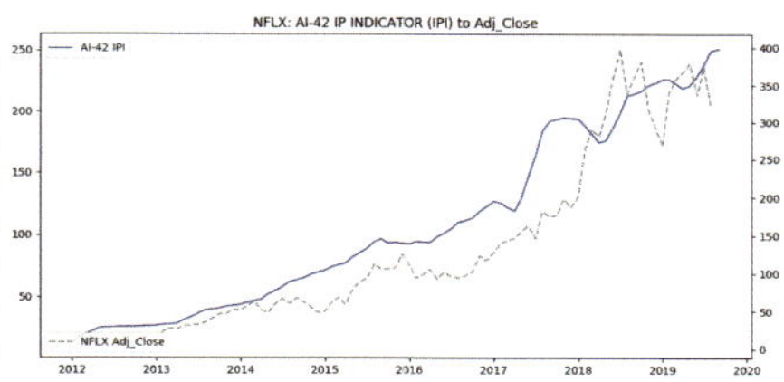
NFLX: AI-42 IP INDICATOR (IPI) to Adj_Close
AI-42 IPI
NFLX Adj_Close

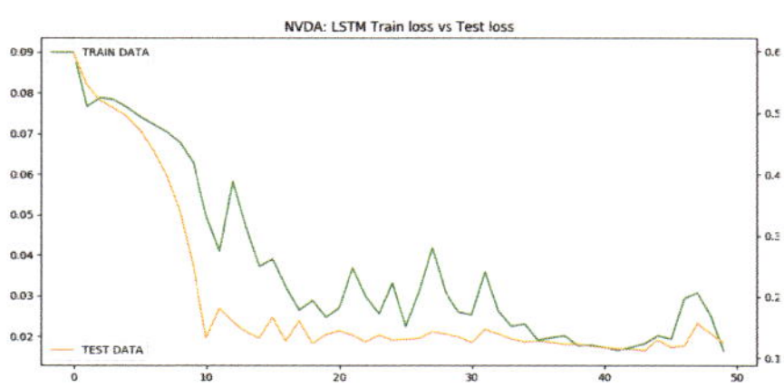
NVDA: LSTM Train loss vs Test loss
TRAIN DATA
TEST DATA

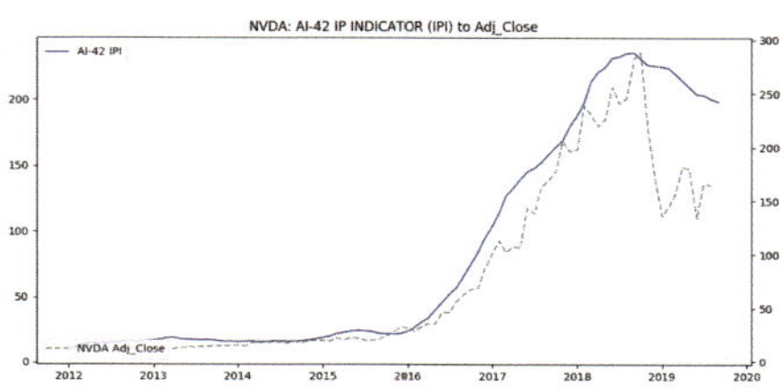
NVDA: AI-42 IP INDICATOR (IPI) to Adj_Close
AI-42 IPI
NVDA Adj_Close

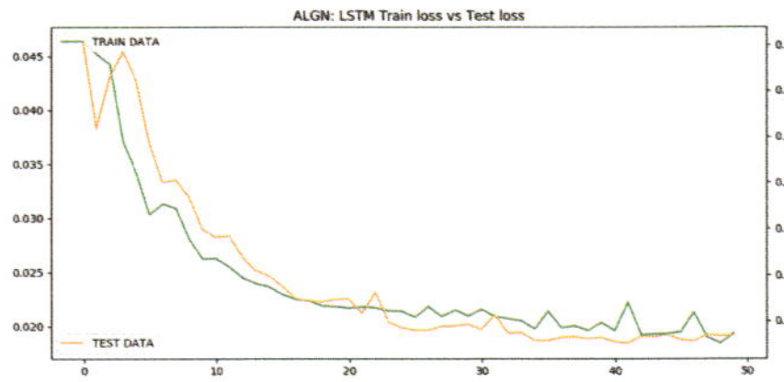
ALGN: LSTM Train loss vs Test loss
TRAIN DATA
TEST DATA

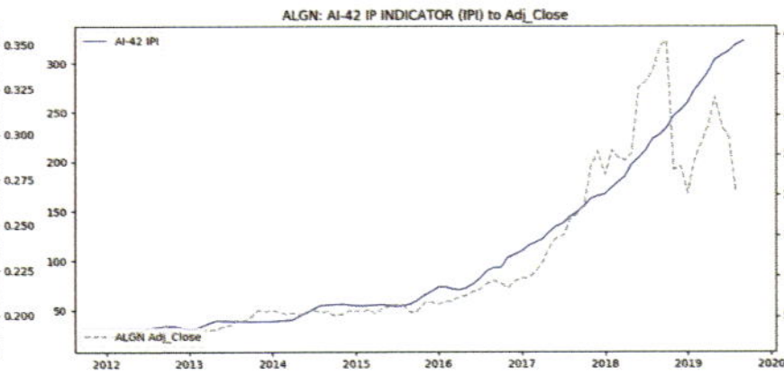
ALGN: AI-42 IP INDICATOR (IPI) to Adj_Close
AI-42 IPI
ALGN Adj_Close

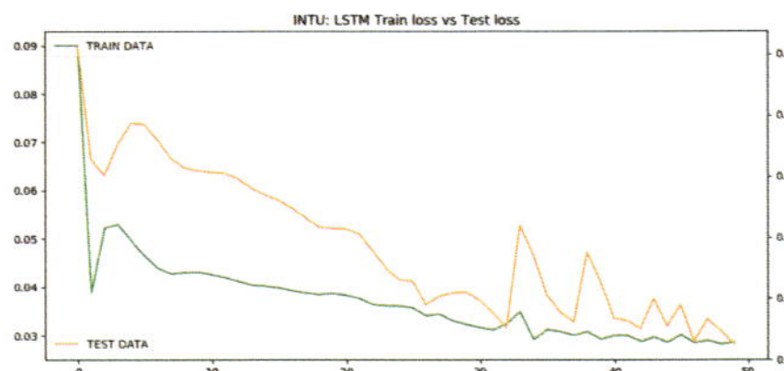
INTU: LSTM Train loss vs Test loss
TRAIN DATA
TEST DATA

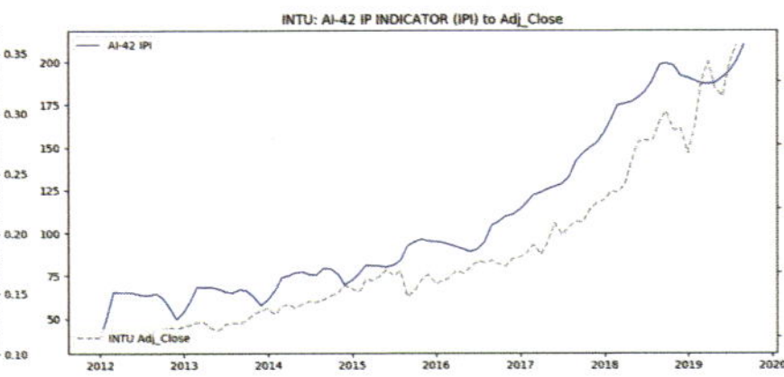
INTU: AI-42 IP INDICATOR (IPI) to Adj_Close
AI-42 IPI
INTU Adj_Close

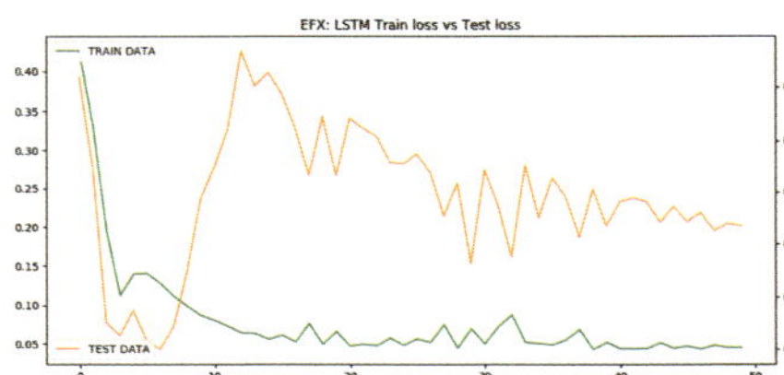
EFX: LSTM Train loss vs Test loss
TRAIN DATA
TEST DATA

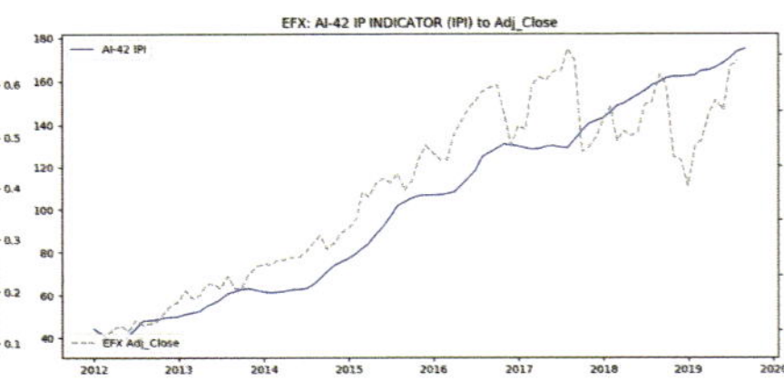
EFX: AI-42 IP INDICATOR (IPI) to Adj_Close
AI-42 IPI
EFX Adj_Close

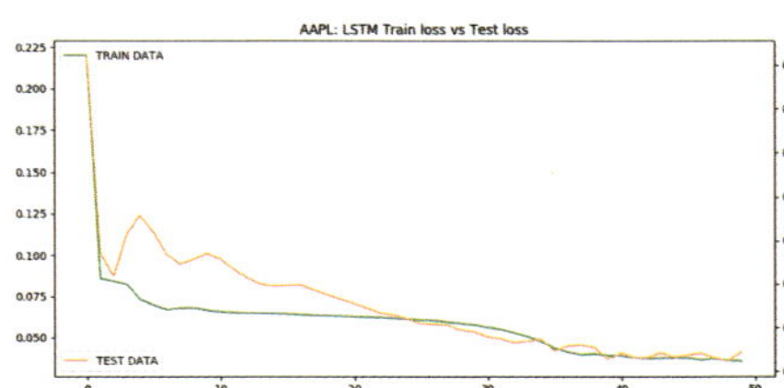
AAPL: LSTM Train loss vs Test loss
TRAIN DATA
TEST DATA

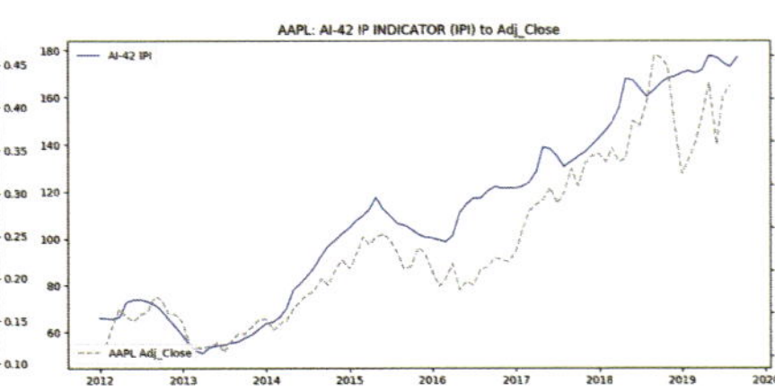
AAPL: AI-42 IP INDICATOR (IPI) to Adj_Close
AI-42 IPI
AAPL Adj_Close

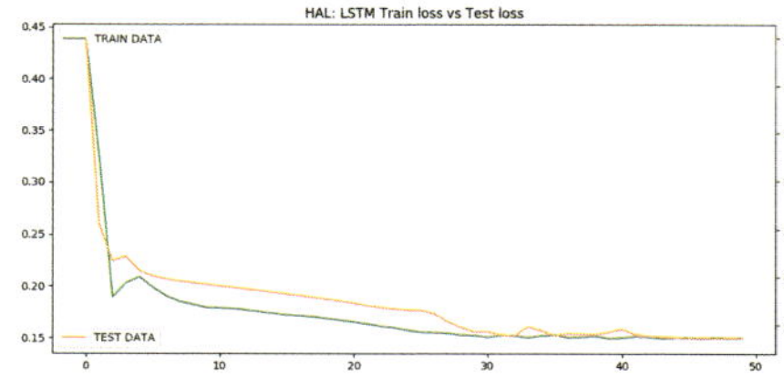
HAL: LSTM Train loss vs Test loss
TRAIN DATA
TEST DATA

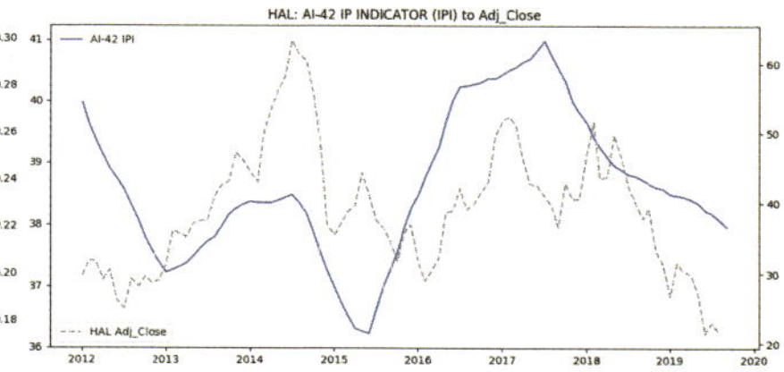
HAL: AI-42 IP INDICATOR (IPI) to Adj_Close
AI-42 IPI
HAL Adj_Close

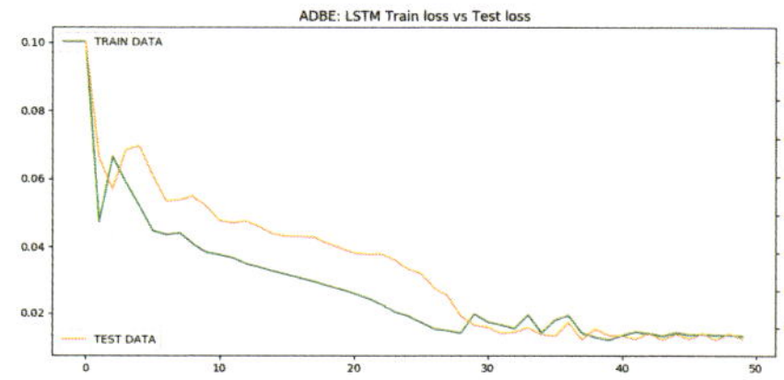
ADBE: LSTM Train loss vs Test loss
TRAIN DATA
TEST DATA

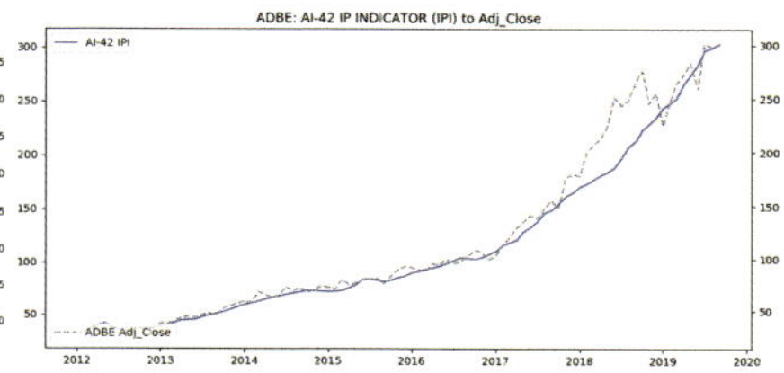
ADBE: AI-42 IP INDICATOR (IPI) to Adj_Close
AI-42 IPI
ADBE Adj_Close

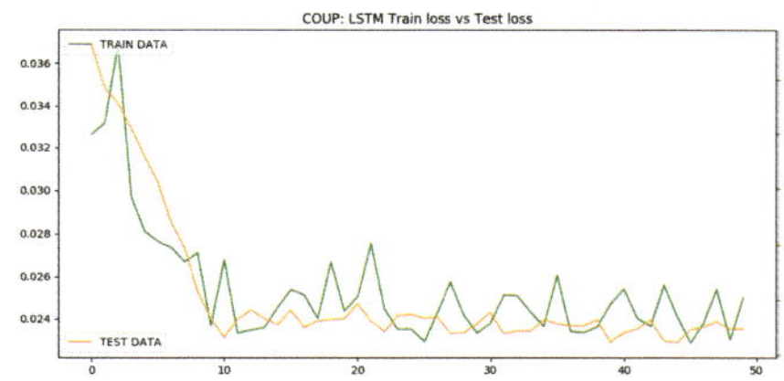
COUP: LSTM Train loss vs Test loss
TRAIN DATA
TEST DATA

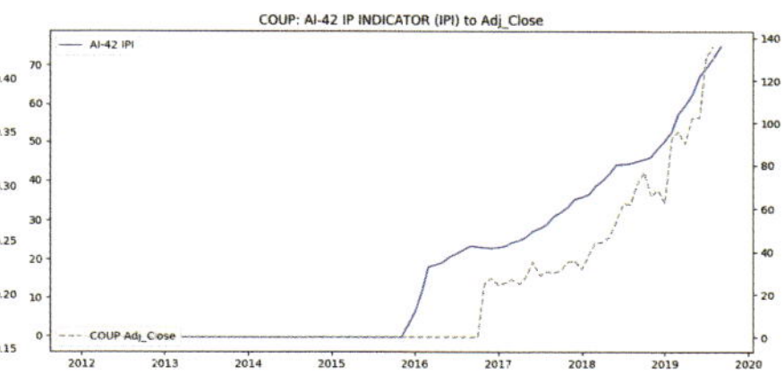
COUP: AI-42 IP INDICATOR (IPI) to Adj_Close
AI-42 IPI
COUP Adj_Close

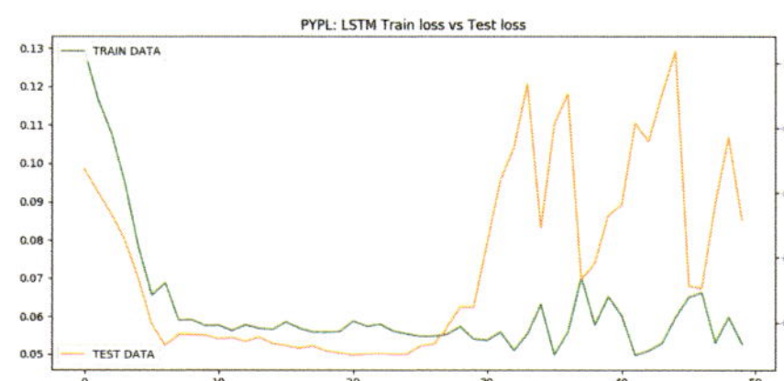
PYPL: LSTM Train loss vs Test loss
TRAIN DATA
TEST DATA

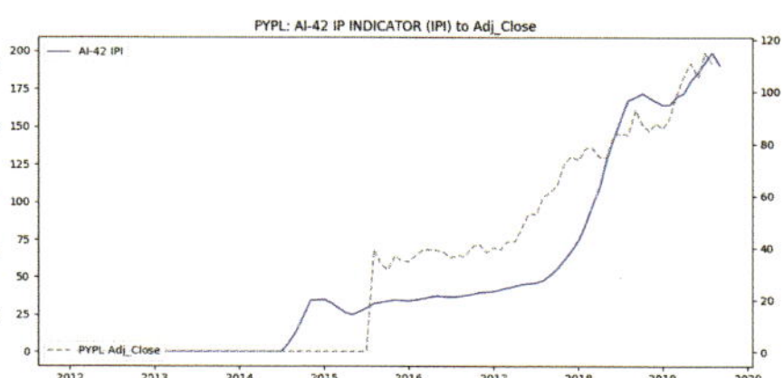
PYPL: AI-42 IP INDICATOR (IPI) to Adj_Close
AI-42 IPI
PYPL Adj_Close

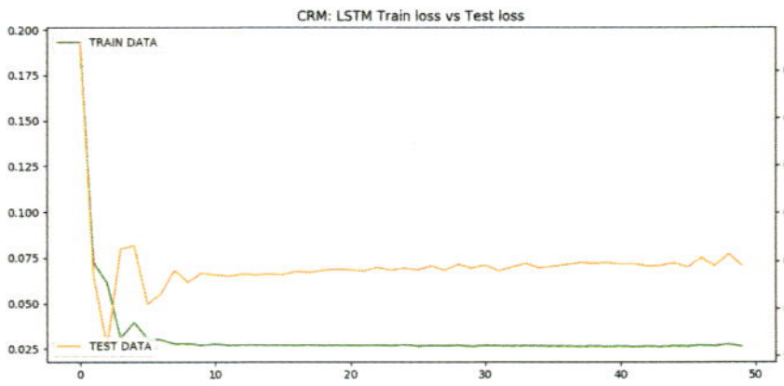
CRM: LSTM Train loss vs Test loss
TRAIN DATA
TEST DATA

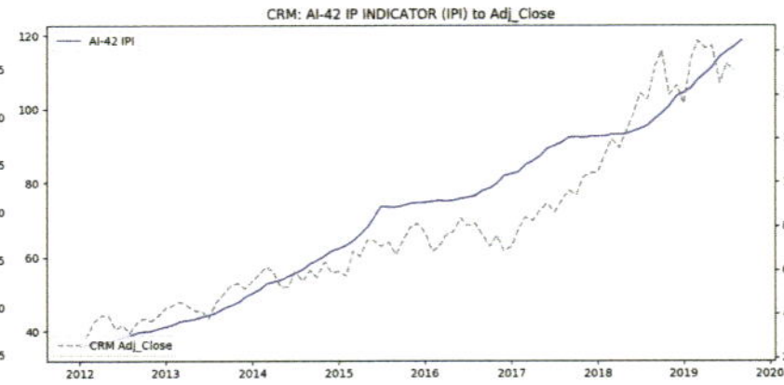
CRM: AI-42 IP INDICATOR (IPI) to Adj_Close
AI-42 IPI
CRM Adj_Close

FICO: LSTM Train loss vs Test loss
TRAIN DATA
TEST DATA

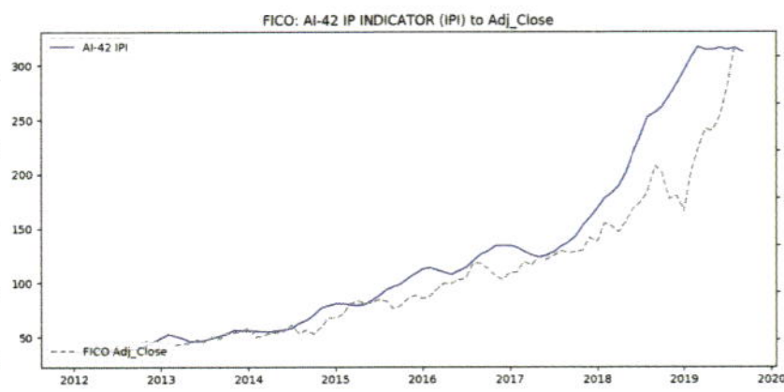
FICO: AI-42 IP INDICATOR (IPI) to Adj_Close
AI-42 IPI
FICO Adj_Close

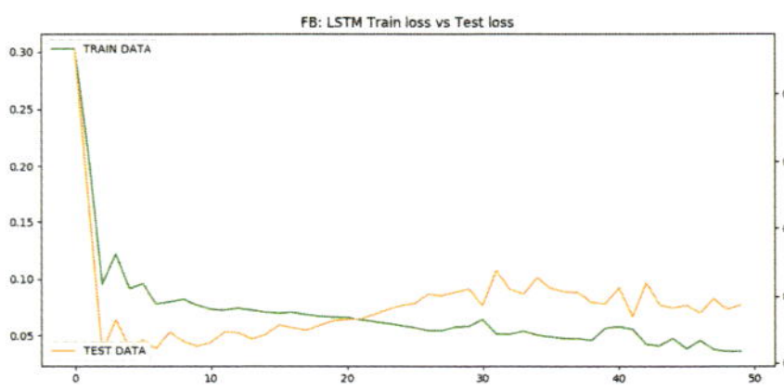
FB: LSTM Train loss vs Test loss
TRAIN DATA
TEST DATA

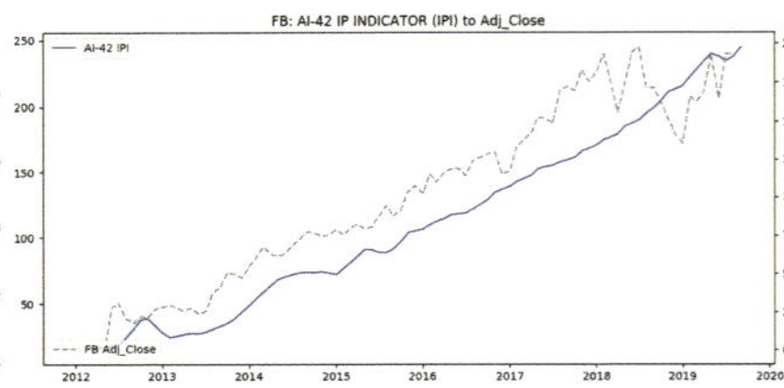
FB: AI-42 IP INDICATOR (IPI) to Adj_Close
AI-42 IPI
FB Adj_Close

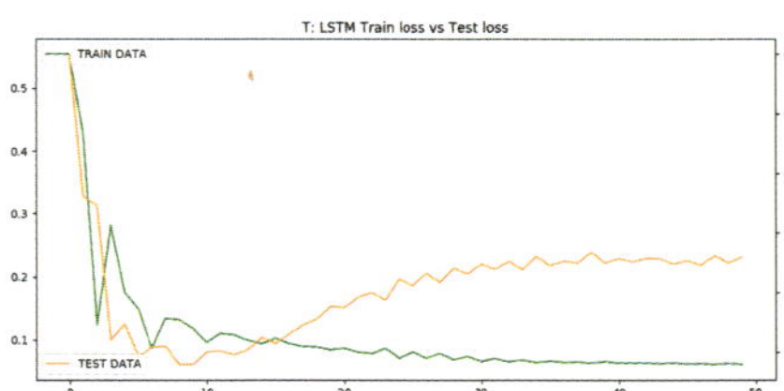
T: LSTM Train loss vs Test loss
TRAIN DATA
TEST DATA

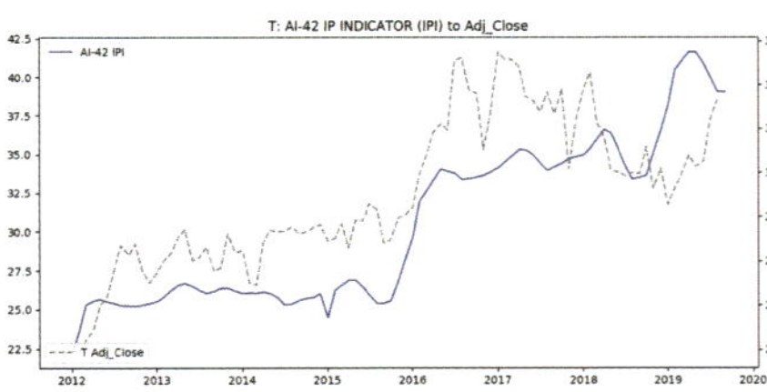
T: AI-42 IP INDICATOR (IPI) to Adj_Close
AI-42 IPI
T Adj_Close

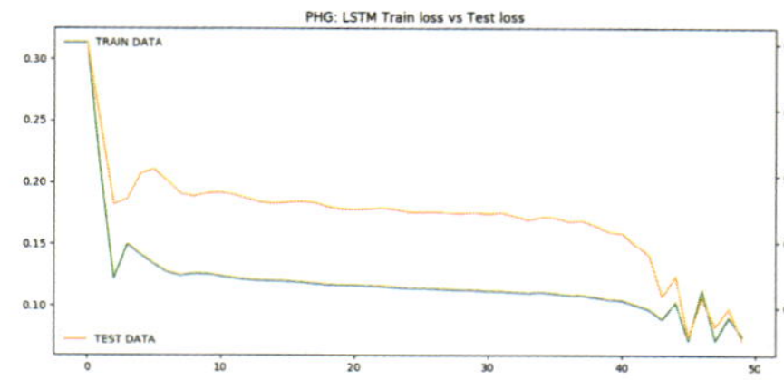
PHG: LSTM Train loss vs Test loss
TRAIN DATA
TEST DATA

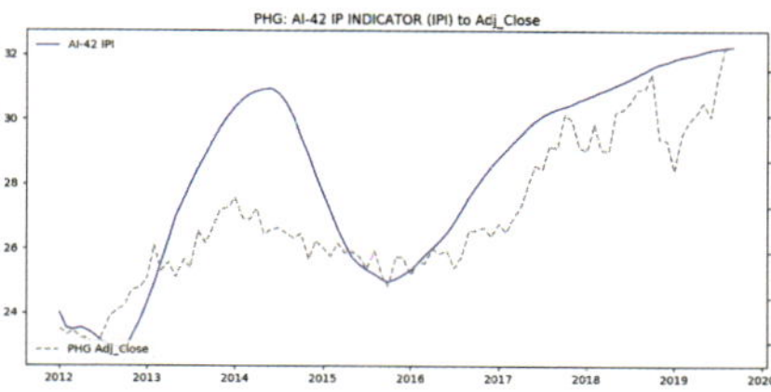
PHG: AI-42 IP INDICATOR (IPI) to Adj_Close
AI-42 IPI
PHG Adj_Close

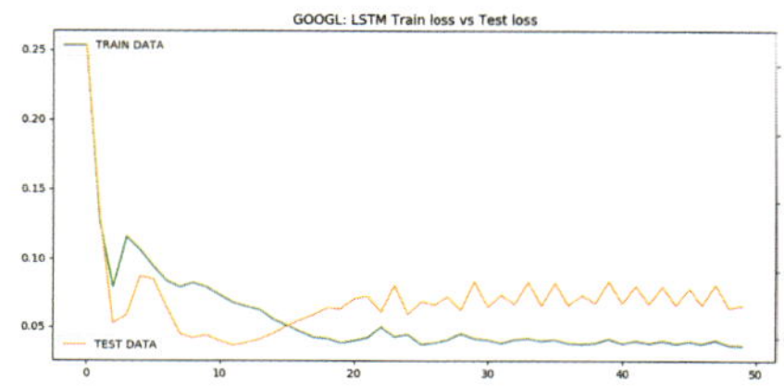
GOOGL: LSTM Train loss vs Test loss
TRAIN DATA
TEST DATA

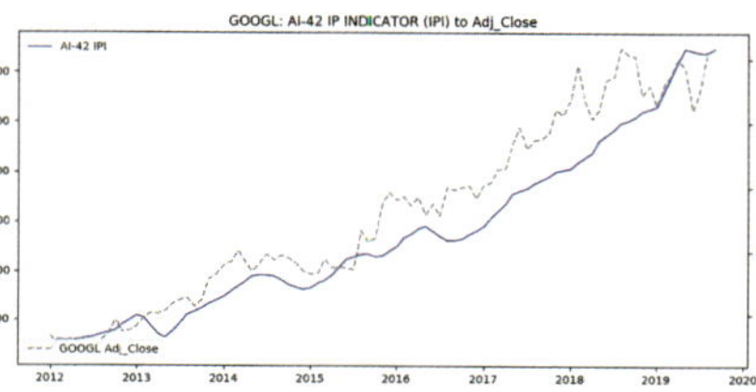
GOOGL: AI-42 IP INDICATOR (IPI) to Adj_Close
AI-42 IPI
GOOGL Adj_Close

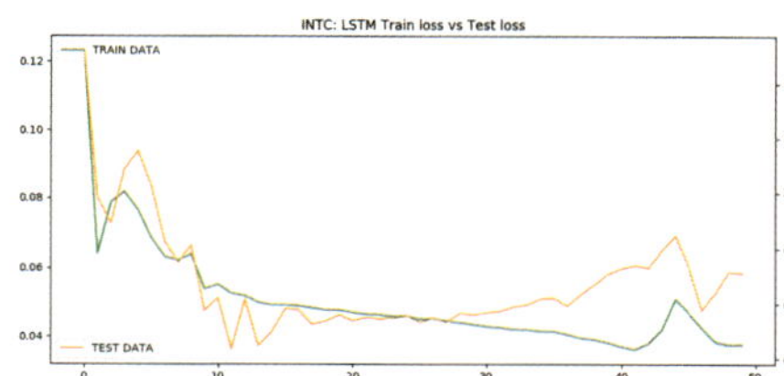
INTC: LSTM Train loss vs Test loss
TRAIN DATA
TEST DATA

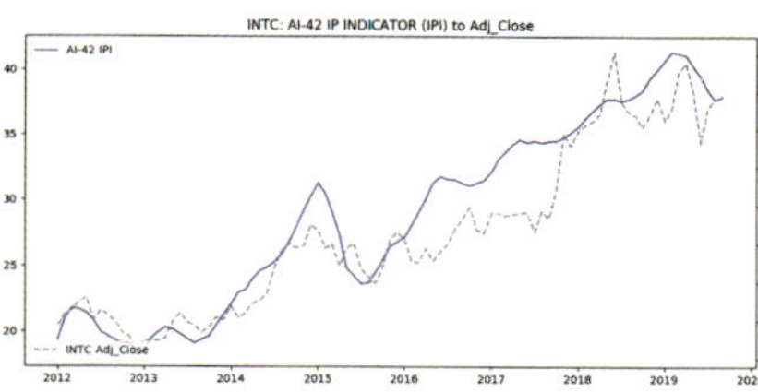
INTC: AI-42 IP INDICATOR (IPI) to Adj_Close
AI-42 IPI
INTC Adj_Close

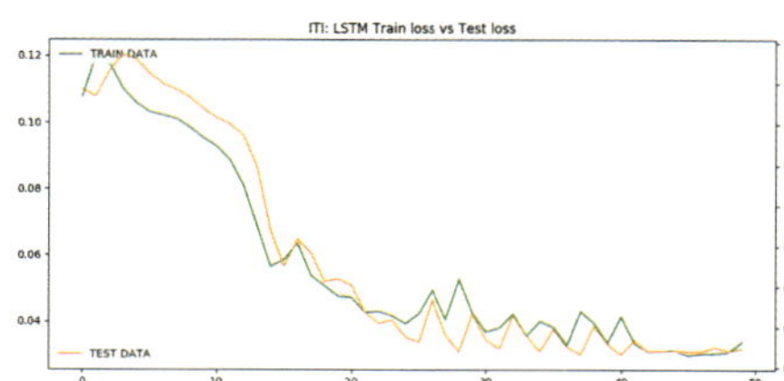
ITI: LSTM Train loss vs Test loss
TRAIN DATA
TEST DATA

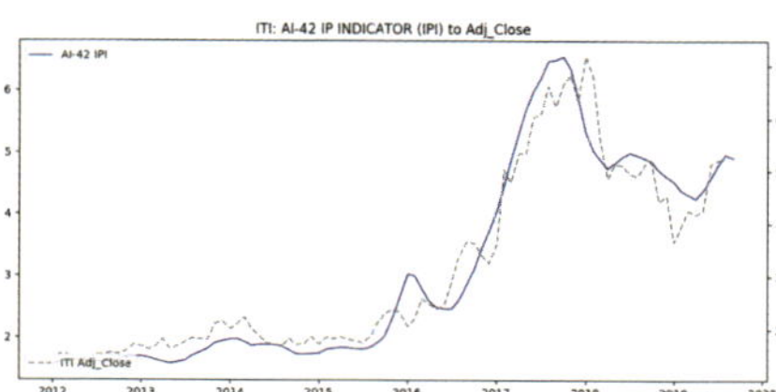
ITI: AI-42 IP INDICATOR (IPI) to Adj_Close
AI-42 IPI
ITI Adj_Close

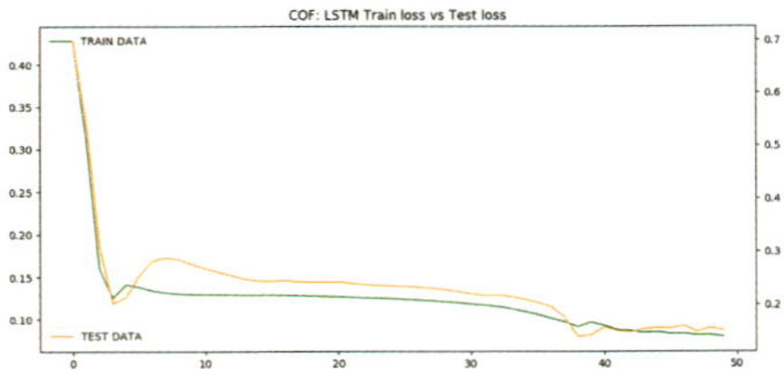
COF: LSTM Train loss vs Test loss
TRAIN DATA
TEST DATA

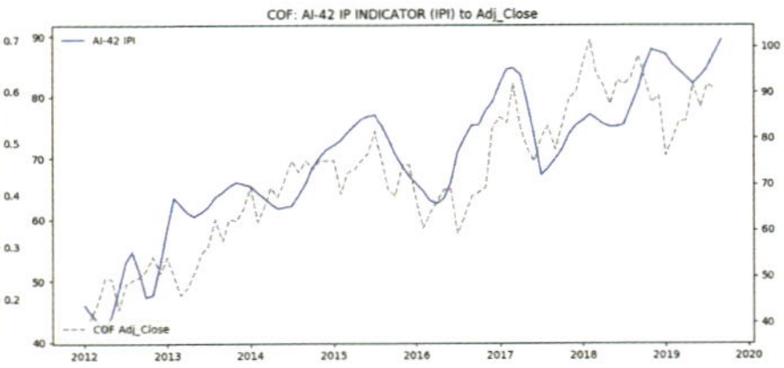
COF: AI-42 IP INDICATOR (IPI) to Adj_Close
AI-42 IPI
COF Adj_Close

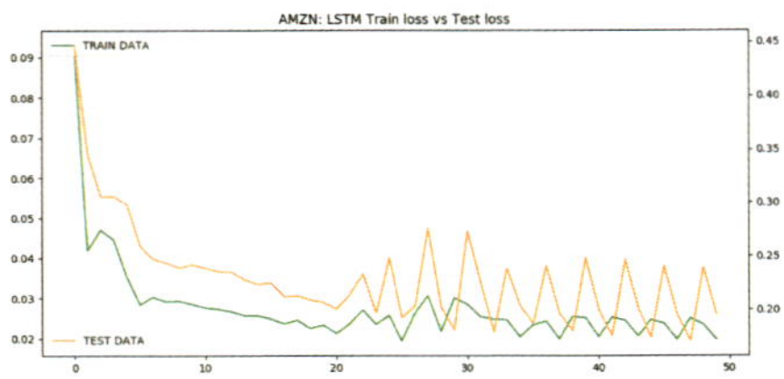
AMZN: LSTM Train loss vs Test loss
TRAIN DATA
TEST DATA

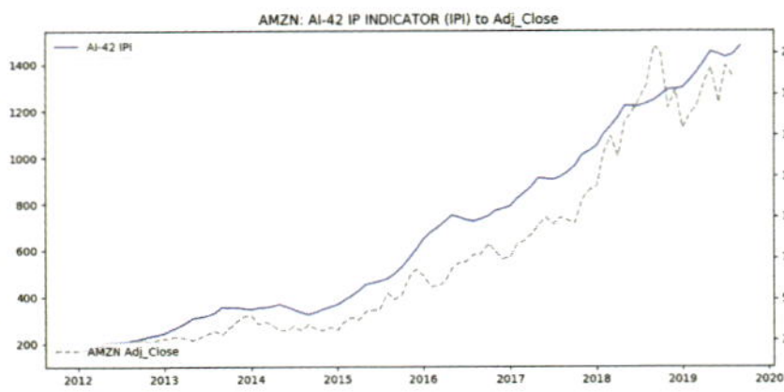
AMZN: AI-42 IP INDICATOR (IPI) to Adj_Close
AI-42 IPI
AMZN Adj_Close

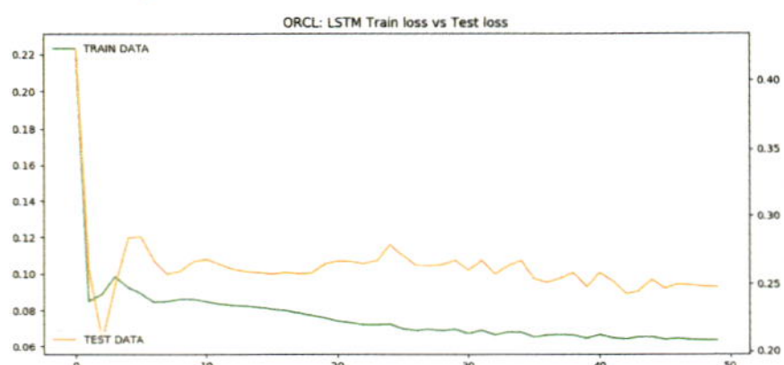
ORCL: LSTM Train loss vs Test loss
TRAIN DATA
TEST DATA

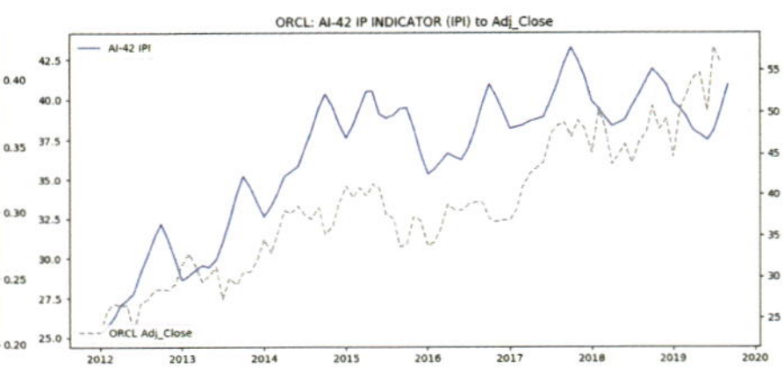
ORCL: AI-42 IP INDICATOR (IPI) to Adj_Close
AI-42 IPI
ORCL Adj_Close

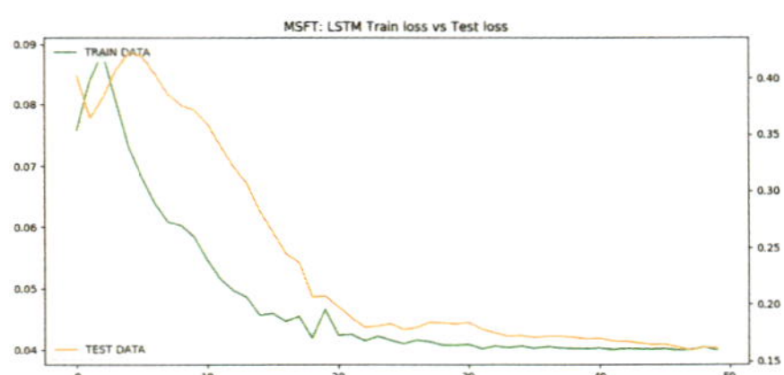
MSFT: LSTM Train loss vs Test loss
TRAIN DATA
TEST DATA

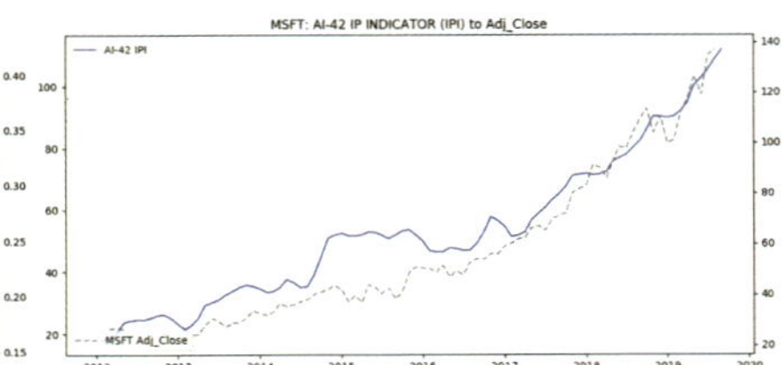
MSFT: AI-42 IP INDICATOR (IPI) to Adj_Close
AI-42 IPI
MSFT Adj_Close

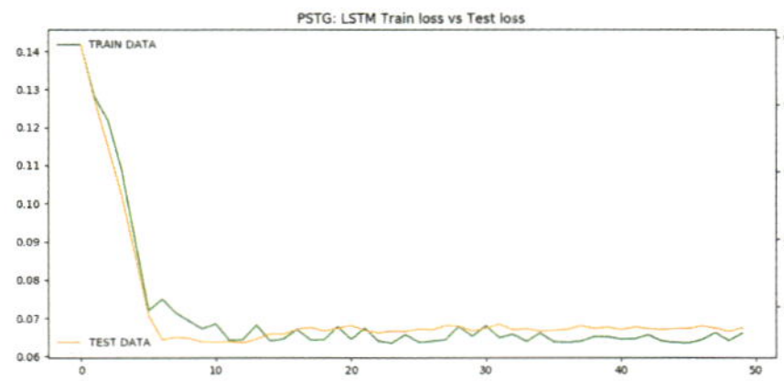

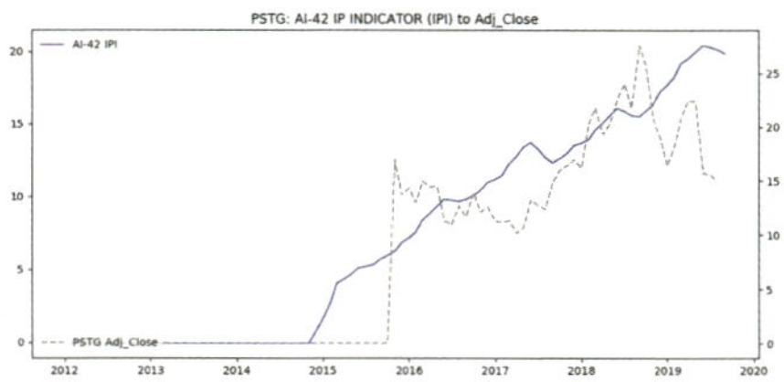

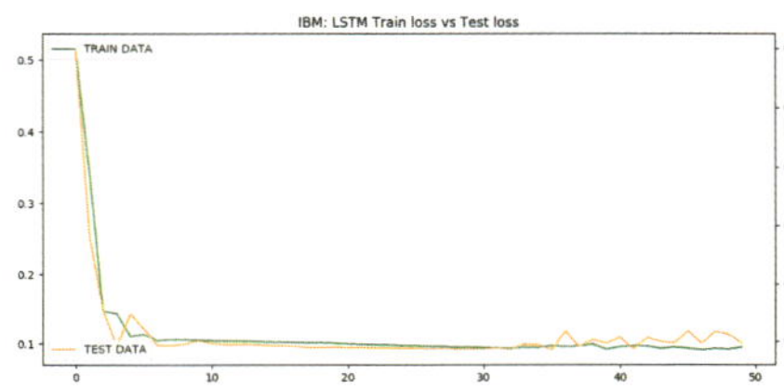

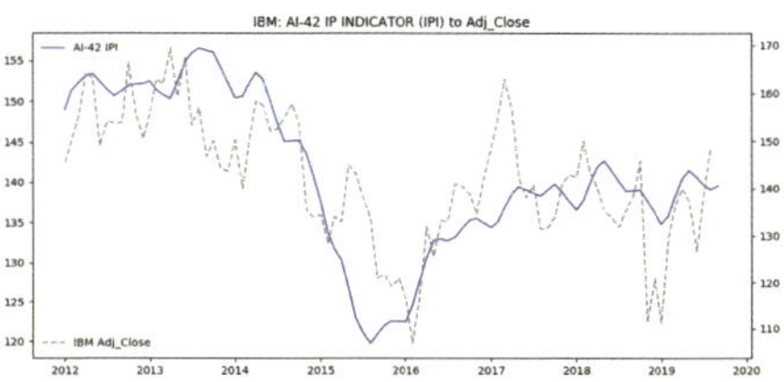

The plots above show: (i) The Mean Absolute Error (MAE) loss on the training and test data of the Long Short-Term Memory (LSTM) recurrent neural network; (ii) the IPI versus its stock price (on an adjusted base not considering stock splits, etc.)

REFERENCES

1. Aalen, O.; Borgan, O.; and Gjessing, H. 2008. Survival and event history analysis: a process point of view. Springer Science & Business Media.
2. Ahuja, G., and Lampert, C. M. 2001. Entrepreneurship in the large corporation: a longitudinal study of how established firms create breakthrough inventions. Strategic Management Journal 22:521– 543.
3. Anthony, B., and Mogee, M. E. 2002. The many applications of patent analysis. Journal of Information Science 28(3):187–205.
4. Bessen, J. 2008. The value of us patents by owner and patent characteristics. 37(5):932–945.
5. Blei, D. M.; Ng, A. Y.; and Jordan, M. I. 2003. Latent dirichlet allocation. 993–1022.
6. Carpenter, M. P.; Narin, F.; and Woolf, P. 1981. Citation rates to technologically important patents. World Patent Information 3(4):160–163.
7. Chakraborty, T.; Kumar, S.; Goyal, P.; Ganguly, S.; and Mukher- jee, A. 2014. Towards a stratified learning approach to predict future citation counts. In JCDL.
8. Deerwester, S.; Dumais, S.; and Harshman, R. 1990. Indexing by latent semantic analysis. 41(6):391.
9. Falk, N., and Train, K. 2016. Patent valuation with forecasts of forward citations. Journal of Business

Valuation and Economic Loss Analysis.

10. Fischer, T., and Henkel, J. 2011. Patent trolls on markets for technology - an empirical analysis of trolls' patent acquisitions. Research Policy 41(9):1519–1533.
11. Fujii, A. 2007. Enhancing patent retrieval by citation analysis. In SIGIR, 793–794.
12. Gompers, P.; Lerner, J.; and Scharfstein, D. 2005. Entrepreneurial spawning: Public corporations and the genesis of new ventures, 1986 to 1999. The Journal of Finance 60(2):577–614.
13. Griliches, Z.; Pakes, A.; and Hall, B. H. 1986. The value of patents as indicators of inventive activity.
14. Griliches, Z. 1990. Patent statistics as economic indicators: A survey. Journal of Economic Literature 28(4):1661–1707.
15. Hall, B. H.; Jaffe, A. B.; and Trajtenberg, M. 2000. Market value and patent citations: A first look. No. w7741, National Bureau of Economic Research.
16. Hall, B. H.; Jaffe, A. B.; and Trajtenberg, M. 2001. The nber patent citation data file: Lessons, insights and methodological tools. Technical report, National Bureau of Economic Research.
17. Han, E., and Sohn, S. 2015. Patent valuation based on text min- ing and survival analysis. The Journal of Technology Transfer 40(5):821–839.
18. Harhoff, D.; Narin, F.; Scherer, F. M.; and Vopel, K. 1999. Ci- tation frequency and the value of

patented inventions. Review of Economics and statistics 81(3):511–515.

19. Harhoff, D.; Scherer, F.; and Vopel, K. 2003. Citations, family size, opposition and the value of patent rights. Research Policy 32(8):1343–1363.
20. Lange, K.; Hunter, D.; and Yang, I. 2000. Optimization trans- fer using surrogate objective functions. J. Comput. Graph. Stat. 9(1):1–20.
21. Layne-Farrar, A., and Lerner, J. 2011. To join or not to join: Examining patent pool participation and rent sharing rules. Inter- national Journal of Industrial Organization 29(2):294–303.
22. Liu, K.; Arthurs, J. D.; Cullen, J. B.; and Alexander, R. T. 2008. Internal sequential innovations: How does interrelatedness affect patent renewal? Research Policy 37(5):946–953.
23. Martinez-Ruiz, A., and Aluja-Banet, T. 2009. Toward the def- inition of a structural equation model of patent value: Pls path modelling with formative constructs. REVSTAT–Statistical Journal 7(3):265–290.
24. Moore, K. A. 2004. Worthless patents. George Mason Law & Economics Research Paper (04-29).
25. Pakes, A., and Schankerman, M. 1984. The rate of obsolescence of patents, research gestation lags, and the private rate of return to research resources. 73–88.
26. Pakes, A. 1984. Patents as options: Some estimates

of the value of holding european patent stocks. Econometrica 54(4):755–84.

27. Ramos, J. 2003. Using tf-idf to determine word relevance in docu- ment queries. In Proceedings of the first Instructional Conference on Machine Learning.
28. Rosenkopf, L., and Almeida, P. 2003. Overcoming local search through alliances and mobility. Management Science 49(6):751– 766.
29. Sapsalis, E.; La Potterie, B. V. P. D.; and Navon, R. 2006. Aca- demic versus industry patenting: An in-depth analysis of what de- termines patent value. Research Policy 35(10):1631–1645.
30. Shen, H.; Wang, D.; Song, C.; and Baraba'si, A. 2014. Mod- eling and predicting popularity dynamics via reinforced poisson processes. In AAAI.
31. Sterzi, V. 2013. Patent quality and ownership: An analysis of uk faculty patenting. Research Policy 42(2):564–576.
32. Trajtenberg, M.; Henderson, R.; and Jaffe, A. 1997. University versus corporate patents: A window on the basicness of invention. Economics of Innovation and New Technology 5(1):19–50.
33. Trajtenberg, M. 1990. A penny for your quotes: patent citations and the value of innovations. The Rand Journal of Economics 172–187.
34. Wang, D.; Song, C.; and Baraba'si, A. 2013. Quantifying long- term scientific impact.

Science 342(6154):127–132.

35. Xiao, S.; Yan, J.; Li, C.; Jin, B.; Wang, X.; Yang, X.; Chu, S.; and Zha, H. 2016. On modeling and predicting individual paper citation count over time. In IJCAI.
36. Xiao, S.; Yan, J.; Yang, X.; Zha, H.; and Chu, S. 2017. Mod- eling the intensity function of point process via recurrent neural networks. In AAAI.
37. Yan, R.; Tang, J.; Liu, X.; Shan, D.; and Li, X. 2011. Citation count prediction: Learning to estimate future citations for litera- ture. In CIKM, 1247–1252.
38. Yan, J.; Xiao, S.; Li, C.; Jin, B.; Wang, X.; Ke, B.; Yang, X.; and Zha, H. 2016. Modeling contagious merger and acquisition via point processes with a profile regression prior. In IJCAI.
39. Yang, S., and Zha, H. 2013. Mixture of mutually exciting pro- cesses for viral diffusion. In ICML.
40. Yu, X.; Gu, Q.; Zhou, M.; and Han, J. 2012. Citation prediction in heterogeneous bibliographic networks. In SDM.
41. Zhou, K.; Zha, H.; and Song, L. 2013a. Learning social infectiv- ity in sparse low-rank networks using multi-dimensional hawkes processes. In AISTATS.
42. Zhou, K.; Zha, H.; and Song, L. 2013b. Learning triggering ker- nels for multi-dimensional hawkes processes. In ICML.
43. Agarwal, V., and N. Naik, 2000, Multi-period

performance persistence analysis of hedge funds, Journal of Financial & Quantitative Analysis 35, 327-342.

44. Agarwal, V., and N. Naik, 2004, Risk and portfolio decisions involving hedge funds, Review of Financial Studies 17, 63-98.
45. Banz, Rolf W., 1981, The relationship between return and market value of common stocks, Journal of Financial Economics 9, 3—18.
46. Brown, Steven J., William N. Goetzmann, Roger G. Ibbotson, and Stephen A. Ross, 1992, Survivorship bias in performance studies, Review of Financial Studies 5, 553-580.
47. Carhart, Mark M., 1997, On persistence in mutual fund performance, Journal of Finance 52, 57—82.
48. Chan, Louis K. C., Josef Lakonishok, and Theodore Sougiannis, 2001, The stock market valuation of research and development expenditures, Journal of Finance 56, 2431-2456.
49. Ciftci, M. and W. Cready, 2010, Scale Effects of R&D as Reflected in Earnings and Returns, working paper, University of Texas at Dallas.
50. Congressional Budget Office, 2005, R&D and Productivity Growth, working paper.
51. Connolly, R.A. and Hirschey, M., 1988, Market value and patents: A Bayesian approach," Economics Letters 27, 83-87.

52. Daniel, K., Grinblatt, M., Titman, S., and Wermers, R., 1997, Measuring mutual fund performance with characteristic-based benchmarks, Journal of Finance 52, 1035- 1058.
53. Daniel, K., and Titman, S., 2006, Market Reactions to Tangible and Intangible Information, Journal of Finance 61, 1605-1643.
54. Eberhart, A., Maxwell, W., and Siddique, A., 2004, An Examination of the Long-Term Abnormal Stock Returns and Operating Performance Following R&D Increases, Journal of Finance 59, 623-650.
55. Fahlenbrach, Rüdiger, 2009, Founder-CEOs, Investment Decisions, and Stock Market Performance, Journal of Financial and Quantitative Analysis 44, 439-466.
56. Fama, E. and MacBeth, J., 1973, Risk, return and equilibrium: empirical tests, Journal of Political Economy 81, 607-636.
57. Fama, Eugene F., and Kenneth R. French, 1992, The cross-section of expected stock returns, Journal of Finance 46, 427—466.
58. Fama, Eugene F., and Kenneth R. French, 1996, Multifactor explanations of asset pricing anomalies, Journal of Finance 51, 55-84.
59. Fung, W., D. Hsieh, N. Nail, and T. Ramadorai, 2009, Hedge funds: Performance, risk, and capital, Journal of Finance 63, 1777-1803.
60. Griffin, John, Patrick Kelly, and Federico

Nardari, 2010, Do market efficiency measures yield correct inferences? A comparison of developed and emerging markets, Review of Financial Studies 23(8), 3225-3277.

61. Griliches, Zvi, 1981, Market value, R&D, and patents, Economic Letters 7, 183-187.
62. Griliches, Zvi, 1984, ed. R&D, Patents and Productivity. Chicago: University of Chicago Press.
63. Griliches, Z., Pakes, A., and Hall, B. H., 1987, The value of patents as indicators of inventive Activity," in P. Dasgupta and P. Stoneman, eds., Economic Policy and Technological Performance, Cambridge, England: Cambridge University Press, 1987.
64. Griliches, Z., A. Pakes, and B. H. Hall, 1991, R&D, patents, and market value revisited: Is there a second (technological opportunity) factor?" Economics of Innovation and New Technology 1, 183-202.
65. Hall, Bronwyn H., 1993a, The stock market's valuation of R&D investment during the 1980's, American Economic Review 83, 259-264.
66. Hall, Bronwyn H., 1993b, Industrial research during the 1980s: Did the rate of return fall? Brookings Papers on Economic Activity Micro 2, 289-344.
67. Hall, Bronwyn H., and Robert E. Hall, 1993, The value and performance of U.S. corporations, Brookings Papers on Economic Activity 1, 1-34.
68. Hall, Bronwyn H., Adam Jaffe, and Manuel

Trajtenberg, 2005, Market value and patent citations, Rand Journal of Economics 36, 16-38.

69. Hall, Bronwyn H., Adam Jaffe, and Manuel Trajtenberg, 2001, The NBER patent citation data file: Lessons, insights, and methodological tools, working paper, NBER.
70. Hirshleifer, David A., Po-Hsuan Hsu, and Dongmei Li, 2010, Innovative efficiency and stock returns, Working paper, UC-Irvine.
71. Hou, K., 2007, Industry information diffusion and the lead-lag effect in stock returns, Review of Financial Studies 20(4), 1113.
72. Huberman, G. and Regev, T., 2001, Contagious speculation and a cure for cancer: a nonevent that made stock prices soar, Journal of Finance 56, 387-396.
73. Ince, Ozgur S., and R. Burt Porter, 2006, Individual equity return data from Thomson Datastream: Handle with care!, Journal of Financial Research 29, 483-479.
74. Jaffe, A., 1986, Technological opportunity and spillovers of R&D: Evidence from firms patents, profits, and market value, American Economic Review 76, 984-1001.
75. Jegadeesh, N., 1990, Evidence of predictable behavior of security returns, Journal of Finance 45, 881-898.
76. Jegadeesh, N., and Titman, S., 1993,

Returns to buying winners and selling losers: Implications for stock market efficiency, Journal of Finance 48, 65-91.

77. Jensen, Michael C., 1993, The modern industrial revolution, exit, and the failure of internal control systems, Journal of Finance 48, 831-880.
78. Jones, D. A., 2007, Voluntary disclosure in R&D-intensive industries, Contemporary Accounting Research, 24: 489-522.
79. Kosowski, R., N. Naik, and M. Teo, 2007, Do hedge funds deliver alpha? A Bayesian and bootstrap analysis, Journal of Financial Economics 84, 229-264.
80. Lakonishok, Josef, Andrei Shleifer, and Robert W. Vishny, 1994, Contrarian investment, extrapolation and risk, Journal of Finance 49, 1541-1578.
81. Lev, Baruch, and Theodore Sougiannis, 1996, The capitalization, amortization, and value-relevance of R&D, Journal of Accounting and Economics 21, 107-138.
82. Malkiel, Burton G., 1995, Returns from investing in equity mutual funds 1971 to 1991, Journal of Finance 50, 549-572.
83. National Bureau of Economic Research Patent Data Project, 2010, https://sites.google.com/site/patentdataproject/Home.

84. Pakes, A., On patents, R&D, and the stock market rate of return." Journal of Political Economy 93, 390-409.
85. Porter, Michael E., 1992, Capital disadvantage: America's failing capital investment system, Harvard Business Review 70, 65-82.
86. Rosenberg, Barr, Kenneth Reid, and Ronald Lanstein, 1985, Persuasive evidence of market inefficiency, Journal of Portfolio Management 11, 9—17.
87. Teo, M., 2011, The liquidity risk of liquid hedge funds, Journal of Financial Economics 100, 24-44.
88. Wermers, Russ, 1997, Momentum investment strategies of mutual funds, performance persistence, and survivorship bias, Working paper, University of Colorado.
89. Bronwyn H. Hall, Adam Jaffe, Manuel Trajtenberg, „Market value and patent citations" UC Berkeley, NBER, and IFS UC Berkeley, NBER, and IFS; Department of Economics 549 Evans Hall, UC Berkeley, Berkeley, CA 9472—3880, USA; Tel. 1 510 642 3878;
90. Albert, M.B., Avery, D., Narin, F., and McAllister, P. "Direct Validation of Citation Counts as Indicators of Industrially Important Patents." Research Policy, Vol. 20 (1991), pp. 251-259.
91. Austin, D. "An Event Study Approach to Measuring Innovative Output: The Case of Biotechnology."

American Economic Review,
Vol. 83 (1993), pp. 253-258.

92. Blundell, R., Griffith, R., and van Reenen, J. "Market Share, Market Value, and Innovation in a Panel of British Manufacturing Firms." Review of Economic Studies, Vol. 66 (1999), pp. 529-554.
93. Cohen, W.M., Nelson, R.R., and Walsh, J.P. "Protecting Their Intellectual Assets: Appropriability Conditions and Why Firms Patent or Not?" Working Paper No. 7552, NBER, 2000.
94. Connolly, R.A. and Hirschey, M. "Market Value and Patents: A Bayesian Approach." Economics Letters, Vol. 27 (1988), pp. 83-87.
95. Crepon, B., Duguet, E., and Mairesse, J. "Research, Innovation, and Productivity: An Econometric Analysis at the Firm Level." Economics of Innovation and New Technology, Vol. 7 (1998), pp. 115-156.
96. Giummo, J. An Empirical Examination of the Value of Patented Inventions Using German Employee Inventors' Compensation Records. Ph.D. dissertation, University of California at Berkeley, 2003.
97. Graham, S.J.H. Capturing Value with Secrecy: Three Studies Exploring Firms' Use of Continuation Patenting in Appropriating Returns from Technological Innovation. Ph.D. dissertation, University of California

at Berkeley, 2003.

98. Griliches, Z. "Market Value, R&D, and Patents." Economic Letters, Vol. 7 (1981), pp. 183-187. —, ed. R&D, Patents and Productivity. Chicago: University of Chicago Press, 1984.
99. Hausman, J.A. "Errors in Variables in Panel Data." Journal of Econometrics, Vol. 31 (1986), pp. 93-118.
100. Pakes, A., and Hall, B.H. "The Value of Patents as Indicators of Inventive Activity." In P. Dasgupta and P. Stoneman, eds., Economic Policy and Technological Performance, Cambridge, England: Cambridge University Press, 1987.
101. "R&D, Patents, and Market Value Revisited: Is There a Second (Technological Opportunity) Factor?" Economics of Innovation and New Technology, Vol. 1 (1991), pp. 183-202.
102. Hall, B. H., "The Manufacturing Sector Master File: 1959-1987." NBER Working Paper No. 3366 (1990)
103. "The Stock Market Valuation of R&D Investment during the 1980s." American Economic Review, Vol. 83 (1993a), pp. 259-264.
104. "Industrial Research during the 1980s: Did the Rate of Return Fall?" Brookings Papers on Economic Activity Micro, Vol. 2 (1993b), pp. 289-344.
105. "Innovation and Market Value." In R. Barrell, G. Mason, and M. O'Mahoney, eds., Productivity, Innovation and Economic Performance, Cambridge,

England: Cambridge University Press, 2000.

106. Ziedonis, R.H. "The Patent Paradox Revisited: Determinants of Patenting in the U.S. Semiconductor Industry, 1980-94." Rand Journal of Economics, Vol. 32 (2001), pp. 101-128.

107. Jaffe, A., and Trajtenberg, M. "Market Value and Patent Citations: A First Look." Working Paper No. 7741, NBER, 2000.

108. "The NBER Patent Citations Data File: Lessons, Insights and Methodological Tools." Working Paper No. 8498, NBER, 2001. Reprinted as Chapter 13 in Jaffe and Trajtenberg (2002)

109. Harhoff, D., Narin, F., Scherer, F.M., and Vopel, K. 1999. "Citation Frequency and the Value of Patented Inventions," The Review of Economics and Statistics 81(3): 511-515.

110. Jaffe, A. "Technological Opportunity and Spillovers of R&D: Evidence from Firms' Patents, Profits, and Market Value." American Economic Review, Vol. 76 (1986), pp. 984-1001.

111. Trajtenberg, M. Patents, Citations and Innovations: A Window on the Knowledge Economy. Cambridge: MIT Press, 2002.

112. Fogarty, M. "The Meaning of Patent Citations: Report of the NBER/Case Western Reserve Survey of Patentees." Working Paper No. 7631, NBER, 2000. Reprinted as Chapter 12 in Jaffe and Trajtenberg (2002).

113. Henderson, R. “Geographic Localization of Knowledge Spillovers as Evidenced by Patent Citations.” Quarterly Journal of Economics, Vol. 108 (1993), pp. 577-598.

114. Kortum, S. and Lerner, J. “Stronger Protection or Technological Revolution: What is Behind the Recent Surge in Patenting?” Carnegie-Rochester Conference Series on Public Policy, Vol. 48 (1998), pp. 247- 304.

115. Lanjouw, J.O. and Schankerman, M. “Patent Quality and Research Productivity: Measuring Innovation with Multiple Indicators.” Economic Journal, forthcoming.

116. Office of Technology Assessment and Forecast (OTAF). U.S. Department of Commerce, Patent and Trademark Office, Sixth Report. Washington, DC: US Government Printing Office, 1976.

117. Pakes, A. “On Patents, R&D, and the Stock Market Rate of Return.” Journal of Political Economy, Vol. 93 (1985), pp. 390-409.

118. “Patents as Options: Some Estimates of the Value of Holding European Patent Stocks.” Econometrica, Vol. 54 (1986), pp. 755-784.

119. Schankerman, M. “The Rate of Obsolescence of Patents, Research Gestation Lags, and the Private Rate of Return to Research Resources.” In Z. Griliches, ed., R&D, Patents, and Productivity, Chicago: University of Chicago Press, 1984.

120. Quillen, C.D., Jr. and Webster, O.H. 2001. “Continuing Patent Applications and Performance of the U.S. Patent Office.” Federal Circuit Bar Journal,

Vol. 11 (2001), pp. 1-21.

121. Scherer, F.M. "Firm Size, Market Structure, Opportunity, and the Output of Patented Innovations." American Economic Review, Vol. 55 (1965), pp. 1097-1123.

122. Schmookler, J. Invention and Economic Growth. Cambridge: Harvard University Press, 1966. Scotchmer, S. "Standing on the Shoulders of Giants: Cumulative Innovation and the Patent Law." Journal

123. of Economic Perspectives, Vol. 5 (1991), pp. 29-41. Shane, H. "Patent Citations as an Indicator of the Value of Intangible Assets in the Semiconductor

124. Industry." Photocopy, The Wharton School, University of Pennsylvania, 1993. Trajtenberg, M. "A Penny for Your Quotes: Patent Citations and the Value of Innovations." Rand Journal of Economics, Vol. 21 (1990), pp. 172-187.

125. Henderson, R., and Jaffe, A. "University versus Corporate Patents: A Window on the Basicness of Invention." Economics of Innovation and New Technology, Vol. 5 (1997), pp. 19-50

ABOUT THE AUTHOR

Daniel Mattes is an Austrian Internet entrepreneur and business angel. He is the founder and CEO of Artificial Intelligence company "42" and a judge and business angel on the Austrian television show '2 Minuten 2 Millionen', the Austrian version of Shark Tank, which airs on Puls4.

His AI market intelligence company "42" focuses on becoming an independent AI authority by analysing the entire AI ecosystem and by providing individual company ratings which are generated with a combined quantitative and qualitative approach by combining big data analytics and an established expert board. 42 is also publishing the AI equivalent of the DJIA index, the "AI-42 Index", expressing the global growth of the most promising companies in the field of Artificial Intelligence. The company is based in London, UK.

Prior to 42, in 2010, he founded Jumio, an online authentication company, which became the market leader with 3500+ employees quickly. Prior to Jumio, in 2005, he founded VoIP company Jajah, which was acquired 2009 for $207 million by Telefónica. In 2007, he was voted 81st most important Austrian citizen by Austrian magazine "News" in the "1000 most important Austrians" list.

»THE ESSENCE OF THE COSMOS IS THE NUMBER.«

Pythagoras of Samos (c.570 – c.495 BC)
ancient Ionian Greek philosopher, mathematician
and the eponymous founder of Pythagoreanism.